GUIDE TO ESSENTIAL BIOSTATISTICS

IN AGCHEM AND BIOSCIENCE R&D

HARRY TEICHER

BIOCOMM

"The scientist is not a person who gives the right answers, he is one who asks the right questions."

- CLAUDE LEVI-STRAUSS (FRENCH ANTHROPOLOGIST)

ABOUT THIS BOOK

———

GUIDE TO ESSENTIAL BIOSTATISTICS is the third book in the LABCOAT GUIDE TO CROP PROTECTION series.

Aimed at managers, researchers, and others looking for an overview of essential principles of Biostatistics, this book is an easily accessible primer for scientists and research workers not trained in mathematical theory, but who have previously followed a course in Biological Statistics.

This book provides a readily accessible overview on how to plan, implement and analyze experiments without access to a dedicated staff of statisticians. It contains few calculations (the "how" of Biostatistics) but instead provides an overview of the "why" - what is it the numbers are telling us, and how can we use this to plan trials, understand our data and make decisions.

Designed to fit in a lab coat pocket for easy access, this GUIDE TO ESSENTIAL BIOSTATISTICS compiles some of the most-used "quick-and-dirty" Biostatistical techniques, approximations and rules-of-thumb used in the design and analysis of biological experiments.

———

ABOUT THE AUTHOR

———

Harry Teicher is a Crop Protection Scientist and Plant Biochemist, providing independent Strategic R&D Management, Scientific & Communications solutions to AgChem and BioScience Organizations developing science-based products.

He has more than 20 years of Conventional & Biological AgChem R&D experience, with more than 10 years as Study Director providing biological & registration support for commercial crop protection products.

Harry Teicher is an Administrator of the INSEAD Strategic R&D Management Alumni Network LinkedIn group. Follow him on LinkedIn, Twitter and Facebook.

For more information:
www.biocomm.eu
teicher@biocomm.eu

BOOKS BY HARRY TEICHER

Starting a new Crop Protection project or starting a new role – the LABCOAT GUIDE TO CROP PROTECTION series will help you focus on specific topics and get you up to speed fast!

Available in eBook and Print formats at:

https://biocomm.eu/crop-protection-books/

PESTICIDES & BIOPESTICIDES: FORMULATION & MODE OF ACTION is the first book in the LABCOAT GUIDE TO CROP PROTECTION series - this book is an easily accessible introduction to essential principles of Pesticide and Biopesticide Mode Of Action and Formulation.

STRATEGIC R&D MANAGEMENT: AGCHEM & BIOSCIENCE is the second book in the LABCOAT GUIDE TO CROP PROTECTION series - this book is an easily accessible introduction to essential principles of Strategic R&D Management.

ESSENTIAL BIOSTATISTICS is the third book in the LABCOAT GUIDE TO CROP PROTECTION series - this book is an easily accessible primer for scientists and research workers not trained in mathematical theory, but who have previously followed a course in Biological Statistics.

ONLINE COURSES

Are you starting a new Crop Protection project, moving teams, or starting a new role - BIOSCIENCE SOLUTION'S ACADEMY course series will provide an easily accessible introduction to specific topics and get you up to speed fast!

These courses are relevant to anyone involved in Crop Protection R&D, including Corporate and Academic Researchers, R&D Managers, Registration Specialists, Product Managers, Business Analysts and Investors.

Available online at:

https://bioscience_academy.teachable.com/

ABOUT BIOSCIENCE SOLUTIONS

BIOCOMM.EU

SCIENTIFIC & STRATEGIC R&D MANAGEMENT
SCIENCE COMMUNICATIONS

———

Started in 2002 by Harry Teicher, BioScience Solutions provides Strategic R&D Management and Support as well as Communications solutions to organizations developing science-based products.

———

Visit our website at: biocomm.eu

CONTENTS

I AM NOT A STATISTICIAN!

The information presented here comprises approximations and rules of thumb which have proven useful in designing and analyzing non-critical trials.

For critical trials, ALWAYS seek the advice of a qualified statistician.

INTRODUCTION

During the more than 20 years I have spent in Crop Protection research and research management, I came to realize that while I and many of my colleagues had followed the same courses in biostatistics, very few of us could apply the methods we had learnt, or analyze and understand the data generated, without repeatedly referring to our textbooks.

In addition, it soon became apparent that very few of the methods we had learnt were sufficient to analyze the majority of our trials.

To address these issues, I prepared a series of internal courses in these most-used "quick-and-dirty" techniques, approximations and rules-of-thumb for my laboratory colleagues, and these courses proved so popular I was asked to compile them as a printed manual.

The result is presented in this book - aimed at scientists and research workers not necessarily trained in mathematical theory, but who have previously followed a course in Biological Statistics, and who need a readily accessible overview on how to plan, implement and analyze "day-to-day" experiments without access to a dedicated staff of statisticians.

It contains few calculations (the "how" of biostatistics) but instead provides an overview of the "why" - what is it the numbers are telling us, and how can we use this to plan trials, understand our data and make decisions. It is designed to fit in a lab coat pocket for easy access to enough information to allow us to be better prepared than 90% (±5%) of our colleagues!

INTRODUCTION

As my background is in plant biology and crop protection, I use examples from the agricultural sciences. The biostatistical tests, approximations and rules of thumb described are however applicable to many other branches of biological experimentation.

———

A SHORT HISTORY OF APPLIED BIOSTATISTICS

The first quarter of the 20th century was an intense period of statistical development driven in part by advances in the science of genetics, and in part by the need to develop mathematical methods for the study of heredity and evolution.

It culminated by providing non-mathematical scientists with computationally simple tools for the design and analysis of their experiments based on elementary algebra, rather than on complex matrix functions and integrals.

Most of the statistical methods used by researchers in the biological sciences today stem from the insight of a handful of statisticians, and their interactions.

Four statistical pioneers in particular are immortalized in the distributions and statistical methodologies named after them.

Their influence is so significant to contemporary research in the biological sciences that the history and origins of their insights, statistical distributions and tests - in such common use today - is worth recounting.

English mathematician and biostatistician **Karl Pearson (1857-1936)** is credited with the establishment of modern mathematical statistics.

Among many other contributions to statistics, Karl Pearson introduced the p-value (Chapter 4), or probability value - the probability of finding the observed results when the null hypothesis is true as well as the term "standard deviation" (Chapter 5) in 1894 to replace the earlier "root mean square error" and "error of mean square".

In addition, Karl Pearson created the first volume of statistical tables in "Tables for statisticians and biometricians" (1914).

George Waddel Snedecor (1881-1974) was an American mathematician and statistician, and a pioneer of modern applied (as opposed to mathematical) statistics. Snedecor was dedicated to developing statistical methods for scientists not trained in mathematical theory, facilitating the interpretation of data within the biological sciences.

Snedecor's "Statistical methods applied to experiments in agriculture and biology" (1937) and "Statistical methods" (1938) are considered seminal in the development of applied statistics for research workers.

Perhaps the greatest name in the developing field of applied statistics for the biological sciences is that of British statistician and geneticist **Ronald A. Fisher (1892-1962)**.

Fisher contributed to the design and statistical analysis of experiments for non-mathematical research workers through his position as a statistician at the Rothamsted Agricultural Experiment Station, the oldest agricultural research institute in the United Kingdom.

Fisher's most important contributions to statistical methods include the introduction of the concept of randomization (Chapter 8), and the analysis of variance (ANOVA; Chapter 18) to compare the means of multiple samples, providing solutions to issues of variance arising from factors such as the heterogeneity of soils and the variability of biological material.

Several of his most important contributions were published in "Statistical methods for research workers" (1925).

Fisher focused on the development of methods for small samples (typical for the crop studies carried out at Rothamsted) and identified the distributions of many sample statistics, publishing "The design of experiments" in 1935 and "Statistical tables" in 1947 (following on from Karl Pearson's previously published book of tables.

William Sealy Gosset (1876-1937) was a chemist and statistician hired by the Guinness Brewery to apply biochemistry and statistics to Guinness' industrial processes.

Gosset introduced the z-statistic to test the means of small, normally-distributed samples for quality control in brewing, and published it anonymously under the name "Student" in Biometrika (1908), following a sojourn at Karl Pearson's laboratory in London.

Gosset's test was adapted by Fisher to incorporate the concept of "degrees of freedom" (introduced by him in its statistical context) in a 1924 paper.

Gosset himself appears to have introduced the t-nomenclature (t-distribution; t-test) in correspondence with Fisher. The t-statistic (Chapter 15) is thus also termed Students t-distribution and Students t-test.

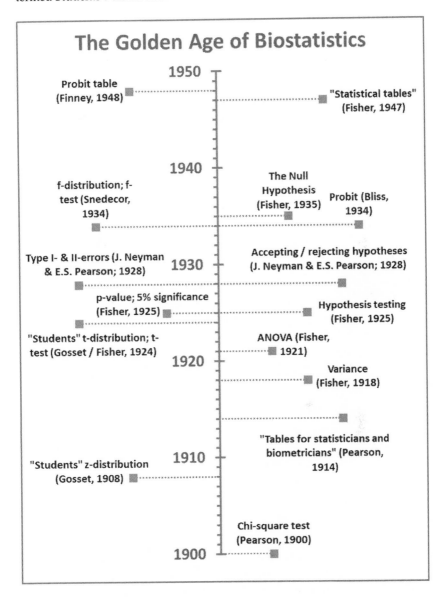

In contrast to Pearson (who sought correlations in large samples), Fisher and Gosset used small samples more typical for agricultural trials and sought causes rather than correlations.

Their differences in statistical approaches lead to increasingly bitter disputes between Pearson and Fisher, leading Fisher to decline the post of chief statistician under Karl Pearson and fortuitously (especially for experimenters in the biological sciences) chose the position as a statistician at Rothamsted instead.

In contrast, Gosset was able to maintain good relations with both Pearson and Fisher - an admirable feat of diplomacy possibly nurtured by his passion for beer... Gosset would go on to become Chief Brewer at Guinness.

Of relevance for the contents of this book, hypothesis testing in its modern form was extensively applied in R.A. Fishers "Statistical methods for research workers" (1925), while the concept of accepting or rejecting hypotheses (Chapter 1) and of Type-I and Type-II error (Chapter 3); originally referred to as "the first source of error" and "the second source of error") were presented by J. Neyman and E.S. Pearson (son of Karl Pearson) in 1928.

Fisher introduced the null hypothesis (Chapter 2) in "The design of experiments" (1935), noting that the normal hypothesis is never proved or established but is possibly disproved in the course of experimentation".

Although the p-value was introduced by Karl Pearson, it was extensively applied and disseminated in R.A. Fishers "Statistical methods for research workers" (1925).

Here, he advocated the 5% significance level (Chapter 4), identifying that 1.96 standard deviations around the mean is the approximate value of the 97.5 percentile point of the normal distribution.

This in turn led to the rule of thumb of two standard deviations for statistical significance in a normal distribution. One cannot help noticing the irony in light of the ongoing (often heated) debate regarding the use of p-values rather than fixed significance levels!

The f-test (Chapter 15) was initially developed by Fisher as the variance ratio (defined as the ratio of explained variance (or between-group variability) to unexplained variance (or within-group variability) in the 1920s.

The f-distribution was subsequently tabulated, and the f-test named, by Snedecor in 1934 as an improved presentation of Fisher's Analysis of Variance, in order to facilitate its interpretation within the biological sciences.

Probit ("probability unit") models (Chapter 19) were developed by American biologist and statistician **Chester Bliss (1899 - 1979)** in 1934, as a convenient method to evaluate dose response in pesticide data.

Probit allowed researchers to convert mortality (effect) percentages to probit values, which approximated a straight line function between the logarithm of the dose and effect which can be analyzed by simple linear regression methods.

The Probit model was further adapted and tabulated at Rothamsted by British statisticians **D. J. Finney (1917 - 2018)** and W. L. Stevens in 1948 to avoid having to work with negative probits in an era before the ready availability of electronic computing.

It is these Probit tables that even today ensure that dose-response fitting to evaluate dose-response relationships may be conveniently performed when statistical software packages are not available, and experimenters do not have a background in mathematics.

It is unlikely that we will again experience a period as dynamic as that of the early 20th century for the advancement of statistical methods in the biological sciences.

We should continue to recognize the contributions of the period's leading statisticians in developing experimental planning and analysis methods capable of driving the advances in Science of the 20th century - methods which are still applicable and in use almost a century later.

———

THE SCIENTIFIC METHOD

The Scientific Method is the mainstay of R&D and provides an objective and systematic approach to experimentation, by minimizing the influence of experimenter bias or prejudice in the form of preconceived notions.

By adhering to the rigorous methodology of the scientific method, experimenters identify and account for errors arising from experimenter bias and fallacies. Bias may be defined as a systematic error affecting objectivity, distorting experimental findings by selecting one outcome above another.

Confirmation bias is an example in which the tendency is to focus on data supporting a hypothesis while suppressing or ignoring data that does not. Other biases include sampling bias (omitting or including groups from the sample), measurement bias (errors in data measurement) and reporting bias (the tendency to report positive results).

In its simplest form the Scientific Method can be broken down into seven phases:

1. OBSERVE. The observation of an interesting phenomenon.

2. QUESTION. The observed phenomenon gives rise to a question.

3. HYPOTHESIZE. An explanatory hypothesis is proposed to explain the phenomenon, conducting background research if necessary.

SCIENTIFIC METHOD SUMMARY

(1) Observation:
The observation of an interesting phenomenon.

(2) Question:
The observed phenomenon gives rise to a question.

(3) Hypothesis:
A hypothesis is proposed to explain the phenomenon, on the basis of background research.

(4) Experiment:
Designing and implementing one or more experiments to test the hypothesis.

(5) Analyse:
Recording observations and analysing the data.

(6) Evaluate:
Concluding whether to accept or reject the hypothesis and communicating the result.

(7) Iterate:
New experiments to test alternative hypotheses or confirm result by repeating experiment.

Figure 1: Summary of the Scientific Method.

4. EXPERIMENT. Designing and implementing one or more experiments to test the hypothesis. Experiments should be designed to minimize possible errors and bias using appropriate scientific controls and randomization.

5. ANALYZE. Recording observations and analyzing the data. Statistical Trial Planning and Data Analysis are key components of the Scientific Method.

6. EVALUATE. Interpret the data, deciding whether to accept or reject the hypothesis. Publish the results and draw conclusions that serve as a starting point for new hypotheses.

7. ITERATE. Running new experiments to test alternative hypotheses if the original hypothesis is not accepted, or iterative experiments to confirm and/or expand our knowledge if the original hypothesis is accepted.

Scientific method example: smartphone charging.

To obtain a more intuitive understanding, let us apply the Scientific Method to an everyday situation - a smartphone that is not charging.

In this process, we will minimize the influence of experimenter bias or prejudice in the form of preconceived notions.

1. Observe

The observation of an interesting phenomenon: Your smartphone has been on the charger all night, but this morning your smartphone was not charged.

2. Question

The observed phenomenon gives rise to a question: Why has my smartphone not charged?

3. Hypothesize

We can hypothesize that IF the smartphone didn't charge THEN the charger is defective. This hypothesis may then be reworded as a *research* or *working* hypothesis.

Accordingly, you could borrow a charger and see if your smartphone charges - you plug in the replacement charger and attach your smartphone. As we will see later, an experiment has an independent as well as a dependent variable.

The *independent variable* (the charger) can be changed or controlled, and the effect it has on the *dependent variable* (the smartphone) can be recorded and analyzed.

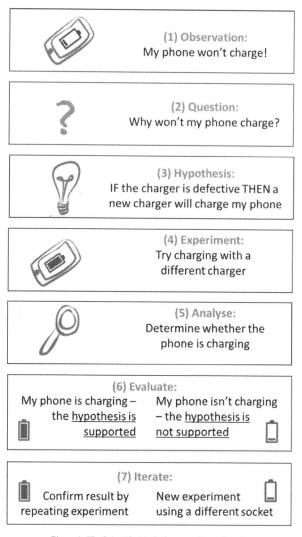

Figure 2: The Scientific Method - smartphone charging.

It is important to change only one variable for an experiment - for example: if we designed an experiment comprising both a replacement charger as well as a replacement smartphone, we would not be able to deduce anything from the data – we would not know if the issue arose from the original charger or smartphone. From this example, we can intuitively understand the importance of a correctly formulated hypothesis.

• • •

5. Analyze

You observe and note whether your smartphone begins to charge on the replacement charger. Ideally, you would repeat this several times to be quite sure of your observations.

In our example, we might repeat the charging process ten times and discover that the replacement charger only charged in eight of these instances.

Don't throw out the observations you think may be wrong - these provide valuable information which might suggest that it is not the charger that is defective but instead may be the socket which is providing intermittent power.

6. Evaluate

If your smartphone charges consistently, then the hypothesis may be considered to be supported. Alternatively, if your smartphone does not charge consistently, then the hypothesis may be rejected.

In practice, however, we can never be sure that the charger functions consistently (for example the socket may only have a 1% misfunction rate, which we would not observe with few replicates).

Thus, although the evidence supports the hypothesis, it does not necessarily mean that the hypothesis is correct. We will consider the implications of this in more detail in the next section.

7. Iterate

If your smartphone charges on the replacement charger, supporting the hypothesis that the original charger is defective, you might propose a new, testable hypothesis: IF the charger is defective THEN the charging tip may need replacing.

Alternatively, if your smartphone does not charge on the replacement charger, you might propose an alternative hypothesis: IF the charger is not effective THEN the power socket may be defective.

The above is a simple example intended to illustrate the steps of the scientific method and provide an intuitive understanding. In R&D the process is far more complicated and requires us to dig a little deeper into the underlying theory.

With this information on the Scientific Method, we are ready to move on to the next section: Proposing a Hypothesis.

I

PROPOSING A HYPOTHESIS

1

HYPOTHESES

Several years ago, I was part of a research team working on the development of herbicide safeners.

Herbicide safeners are (typically) chemicals which protect crops from herbicide injury by accelerating the metabolism of herbicides, or by inhibiting their translocation within plants, facilitating selectivity between crop plants and weed species targeted by the herbicide.

At the time we ran herbicide safener experiments in a dedicated section of the greenhouse which was adjacent to a section containing plants under evaluation for leaf damage (phytotoxicity) as a result of treatment with one of our commercial insecticide products.

We had hit a wall with regard to identifying a formulation additive which could reduce phytotoxicity without reducing insecticidal activity. The project had been placed on hold while we considered our next steps.

Shortly after starting the herbicides safener experiments, we observed that herbicide-treated plants showed the same symptoms of oxidative damage as the adjacent insecticide-treated plants. An idea began to germinate...

According to the precepts of the scientific method, we had made an interesting observation: the symptoms of insecticide phytotoxicity appeared identical to those of oxidative herbicide phytotoxicity.

A quick literature study confirmed that leaf damage by insecticides (phytotoxicity) could in many cases be ascribed to membrane peroxidation arising from reactive oxygen species.

The herbicide safener being tested reduced herbicidal symptoms so effectively that we questioned whether it would be able to reduce the phytotoxicity of the insecticide - perhaps this was the elusive formulation additive which could reduce phytotoxicity without reducing insecticidal activity? We were on our way to developing a hypothesis!

A hypothesis is the basic tenet of the scientific method. It is often described as an "educated guess" to account for an observed phenomenon or a research idea and is based on prior knowledge and observation[1].

A *Research* or *Working* Hypothesis is a proposal or prediction to be proved or disproved through experimentation or observation.

A Research Hypothesis may be formulated using Boolean IF / THEN logic:

IF the charger is defective, THEN a new charger will charge my phone.

IF herbicide safeners prevent herbicide phytotoxicity THEN herbicide safeners could prevent insecticide phytotoxicity.

In the previous section, it was determined that if your smartphone charges consistently, then the hypothesis may be considered to be supported.

In practice, however, we can never be sure that the charger functions consistently (for example the socket may have a 1% malfunction rate, which we would not observe with a few replicates). Thus, although the evidence *supports* the hypothesis, it does not necessarily *prove* that the hypothesis is correct.

A fundamental aspect of the scientific method is Karl Popper's[2] Principle of Falsification: for any hypothesis to be valid, it must be disprovable before it can become accepted as a scientific hypothesis.

Put simply: repeated observations of white swans do not prove the hypothesis that all swans are white, but the observation of a single black swan[3] disproves the hypothesis.

(1) Observation:
Insecticide phytotoxicity appears identical to herbicide phytotoxicity

(2) Question:
Could herbicide safeners reduce insecticide phytotoxicity?

(3) Hypothesis:
IF herbicide safeners reduce herbicide phytotoxicity, THEN herbicide safeners could reduce insecticide phytotoxicity

(4) Experiment:
Treat plants with insecticides in the absence or presence of safeners

(5) Analysis & (6) Statistical Evaluation:

Figure 1.1: Applying the Scientific Method.

Without deviating further down this philosophical rabbit hole, we say that rather than *proving* the working hypothesis, researchers follow the Popperian Scientific method where 'nothing in the sciences can be proven, only disproven'.

Researchers thus work to reject or *disprove* the *Null hypothesis* - the default hypothesis that 'nothing happened'. Researchers also devise an *alternate* hypothesis - one that they think explains a phenomenon - but work to reject the Null hypothesis.

---

1. Hypothesis testing in its modern form was extensively applied in R.A. Fishers "Statistical methods for research workers" (1925), while the concept of accepting or rejecting hypotheses was introduced by J. Neyman and E.S. Pearson (son of Karl Pearson) in 1928.

2. Karl Popper (1902-1994): influential science philosopher, who introduced the concept that science advances by "deductive falsification" *i.e.* experiments *test* theories rather than produce them.
3. Until 1697 when Dutch explorers became the first Europeans to see black swans (*Cygnus atratus*) in Australia, it was presumed - at least by European scientists - that black swans did not exist.

2

THE NULL HYPOTHESIS

The *Null hypothesis* **(H0)**, is the hypothesis that the data generated by an experiment occurred by mere chance and was not affected by the treatment - "nothing happened".

The *alternative hypothesis* **(H1)** is the hypothesis that the treatment influenced the data generated, "something *did* happen".

So, for our herbicides safener case an appropriate research question was: *could herbicide safeners effectively reduce insecticide phytotoxicity?*

From this a Research hypothesis could be formulated: *"IF herbicide safeners reduce herbicide phytotoxicity, THEN herbicide safeners could reduce insecticide phytotoxicity"*, and the associated Null hypothesis and its alternate may take the form:

Null hypothesis (H0): There is no difference between treatments.

Alternative hypothesis (H1): There is a difference between treatments.

Following experimentation and the statistical evaluation of whether the Null hypothesis provides a valid explanation of the data, the Null hypothesis may be rejected or accepted *with a certain level of probability, or confidence* (for example, 95% confidence - more on this later).

Null Hypothesis:
There is <u>NO</u> difference between the safened and unsafened treatments

The **NULL HYPOTHESIS** is a hypothesis which the researcher tries to disprove (nullify)

Alternative Hypothesis:
There <u>IS</u> a difference between the safened and unsafened treatments

The **ALTERNATIVE HYPOTHESIS** is a hypothesis which the researcher tries to prove

Figure 2.1: The Null Hypothesis.

This element of probability arises because we are generally not able to test the entire population and work with samples instead, which brings in a "black swan" element of probability.

Thus, we speak of "rejecting the Null hypothesis in favor of the alternative hypothesis, and "failing to reject the Null hypothesis" rather than of "accepting the Null hypothesis", as we have no way of proving that the data occurred by chance[1].

Similarly, *"failed to prove the prisoner is guilty"* is not the same as *"proved the prisoner is innocent"*.

In the example below, if there is a difference between the safened and unsafened treatments, we reject the Null hypothesis that "nothing happened" and shift our belief to the alternate hypothesis that "something *did* happen" (although the latter has not been proven).

With this information on the Scientific Method and Hypotheses, we are ready to move on to the next section: Designing and implementing experiments (Significance, Power and Effect).

(1) Observation:
Insecticide phytotoxicity appears identical to herbicide phytotoxicity

(2) Question:
Could herbicide safeners reduce insecticide phytotoxicity?

(3) Hypothesis:
IF herbicide safeners reduce herbicide phytotoxicity, THEN herbicide safeners could reduce insecticide phytotoxicity

Null Hypothesis:	Alternative Hypothesis:
There is <u>NO</u> difference between the safened and unsafened treatments	There <u>IS</u> a difference between the safened and unsafened treatments

(4) Experiment:
Treat plants with insecticides in the absence or presence of safeners

(5) Analysis & (6) Statistical Evaluation:

There is NO difference between treatments	There IS a difference between treatments
We fail to reject the Null hypothesis (≠ accepting the Null hypothesis)	We reject the Null hypothesis

Figure 2.2: The Scientific Method - herbicide safening.

---

1. R.A. Fisher introduced the null hypothesis in "The design of experiments" (1935), noting that the normal hypothesis is never proved or established but is possibly disproved in the course of experimentation".

II

DESIGNING AND IMPLEMENTING EXPERIMENTS (SIGNIFICANCE, POWER AND EFFECT)

3

TYPE I AND TYPE II ERRORS

To experimentally test a hypothesis *"IF herbicide safeners reduce herbicide phytotoxicity, THEN herbicide safeners could reduce insecticide phytotoxicity,"* we might predict (the Null hypothesis) that there is no difference between the safened and unsafened treatments.

Accordingly, we could perform an experiment in which we treat plants with insecticides in the absence or presence of safeners and observe for differences in phytotoxicity between treatments, for which the Null hypothesis is: There is no difference between treatments.

During experimentation, researchers will be exposed to two types of error related to hypotheses, termed Type-I and Type-II errors (originally[1] termed "the first source of error" and "the second source of error":

A *Type-I error* occurs when the Null hypothesis is rejected, even though it is correct. This is the "flash in the pan" type error, where you believe you have discovered something extraordinary, even though it is not (a "false positive").

A *Type-II error* occurs when the Null hypothesis is not rejected, despite it being false. This is the "one that got away" type error, where you miss out on something that really is extraordinary (a "false negative).

Let us consider our hypothesis for an experiment to determine whether there is a difference in phytotoxicity between two treatments. We can formulate this as:

Null hypothesis: There is no difference between treatments.

Alternate hypothesis: There is a difference between treatments.

In this example, a Type-I error would lead us to reject the Null hypothesis, claiming that there IS a difference between treatments (false positive) when there is none.

A Type-II error would lead us to *not* reject the Null hypothesis, erroneously concluding that there is NOT a difference in phytotoxicity between the treatments.

In an early-stage herbicide discovery project focusing on efficacy, a Type-II error (false negative) can significantly impact progress and potentially allow a competitor to commercialize a valuable compound.

For example, imagine a research team screening various compounds to identify potential herbicides, including a promising compound with strong efficacy against a specific weed species. However, due to a Type-II error, they mistakenly conclude that the compound lacks sufficient efficacy and discard it prematurely.

Meanwhile, a competitor's research team obtains access to the compound and recognizes its potential. They conduct further studies, optimize its formulation, and successfully demonstrate its effectiveness. Consequently, the competitor proceeds to commercialize the herbicide, gaining a competitive advantage in the market.

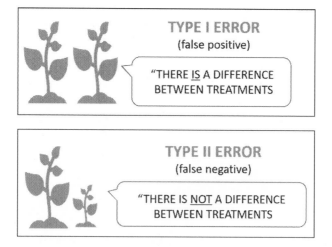

Figure 3.1: Type-I and Type-II errors.

As a result of the Type-II error, the original research team missed the opportunity to recognize the compound's true efficacy and failed to capitalize on its potential.

This can have detrimental consequences for the initial project, as the competitor now has the advantage of a commercially viable herbicide that effectively controls the targeted weed species. The original team may experience setbacks in their research, lose out on potential revenue and market share, and face challenges in catching up with the competitor's success.

In a late-stage herbicide development project focused on efficacy, a Type-I error (false positive) could have significant implications. For instance, imagine a herbicide that has undergone extensive testing and regulatory approvals, with the conclusion that it effectively controls a wide range of weed species.

Due to a Type-I error, the development team mistakenly concludes that the herbicide is highly efficacious against all targeted weeds. As a result, the herbicide moves towards commercialization, and farmers widely adopt it based on the false belief in its effectiveness.

However, if later field trials or real-world applications reveal that the herbicide fails to deliver the expected control against certain weed species, it would be a Type-I error.

The consequences could include crop damage, reduced yields, economic losses for farmers, and loss of trust in the product. Thus, a Type-I error in late-stage herbicide efficacy assessment can have detrimental effects on crop management, farmer livelihoods, and the success of the product.

As we delve into the following chapters, it will become evident that understanding the effects of Type-I and Type-II errors on early-stage discovery and late-stage development projects influences our choices in trial design and the evaluation of trial data.

Recognizing the potential consequences of these errors allows us to make informed decisions that optimize the efficiency and efficacy of our research endeavors.

In the realm of early-stage discovery projects, where the focus lies on identifying novel solutions or opportunities, the risk of a Type-II error (false negative) looms large. By understanding the impact of this error, we become aware of the possibility of missing out on valuable discoveries or dismissing potential breakthroughs prematurely.

Consequently, we can design trials and develop data evaluation methods that are sensitive enough to detect even subtle signals of efficacy or significance, reducing the likelihood of Type-II errors and ensuring that promising leads are thoroughly explored.

Conversely, in late-stage development projects characterized by higher costs and greater emphasis on product viability, a Type-I error (false positive) poses a considerable threat.

The recognition of this error's impact empowers us to approach trial design and data evaluation with a critical eye, striving to minimize the risk of false positives.

We employ more stringent statistical analyses to ensure that any positive findings are truly indicative of efficacy or success. By doing so, we mitigate the potential consequences of Type-I errors, such as wasted resources, misleading conclusions, and misguided decisions regarding the future of the project.

By proactively addressing the specific risks associated with each error, we optimize our chances of identifying valuable discoveries in the early stages and ensuring the reliability of our findings in the later stages.

This understanding ultimately enhances the effectiveness and impact of our research efforts in various domains and facilitates better-informed decisions throughout the project lifecycle.

Assumptions for hypothesis testing	
Type I error (false positive)	Significance (α) 0.05 (5%)
Type II error (false negative)	Power (β) 0.8 (80%)

Although Type I and Type II errors can never be avoided entirely, we can reduce their likelihood. The probability of Type I error is controlled by the significance level (stringency) of the test, denoted by alpha (α), which is typically set at 0.05 (5%).

The probability of Type II error is controlled by the power (sensitivity) of the test, or beta (β), which is typically set at 0.20 (20%) or 80% power.

Two parameters determining appropriate sample sizes will be addressed in the next chapter on *Statistical significance* (for Type-I errors) and *Power* (for Type-II errors).

---

1. The concept of Type-I and Type-II error was originally referred to in 1928 as "the first source of error" and "the second source of error" in papers by J. Neyman and E.S. Pearson (son of Karl Pearson).

4

STATISTICAL SIGNIFICANCE, POWER AND EFFECT SIZE.

In statistical analysis and hypothesis testing, the concepts of significance, variability and effect size play crucial roles in determining the power or sensitivity of a test.

Power refers to the ability of a statistical test to detect a true difference or effect if it exists in the population being studied.

The interplay between effect size, variability, significance, and power determines the sensitivity of a statistical test to detect differences between treatments.

In Figure 4.1, the relationship between effect size, variability, and the ability to differentiate treatments is depicted. When the effect size is suitably large, even if there is substantial variability within the treatments, the treatments can be easily differentiated, making it less challenging to detect a true difference or effect if it exists.

However, as the effect size decreases (a smaller difference between treatments), data overlap increases, and it becomes more challenging to differentiate between the treatments. The statistical test needs to be more sensitive to detect the smaller effect size accurately.

The sensitivity or power of the trial becomes crucial in such cases. A test with higher power is more likely to identify the difference between treatments, even when the effect size is small and the variability is large.

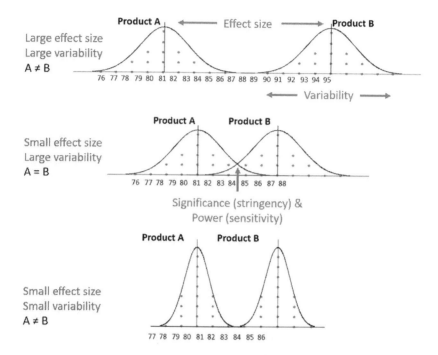

Figure 4.1: The relationship between effect size, variability, and the ability to differentiate treatments.

Significance (stringency)

The significance level of an experiment, called α (alpha) is the probability of rejecting our Null-hypothesis even though it is true, thus concluding that there is a difference between treatments, even though there is none.

The **significance level (α)**, is the probability of rejecting the null hypothesis when it is actually true. For a significance level of 0.05 (or 5%), there is a 5% chance of mistakenly rejecting it and concluding that there is a significant effect or difference (false positive). A small difference in efficacy between two treatments may be statistically significant, but this difference may be too small to make it commercially meaningful!

A lower significance level means that the test is more stringent and less likely to reject the null hypothesis, leading to lower power.

Conversely, a higher significance level means that the test is less stringent and more likely to reject the null hypothesis, leading to higher power.

This is of importance for biological trials where we as researchers are biased toward the conclusion that our experiments support the hoped-for effect - the alternative hypothesis.

Let us consider our proposed experiment in which plants sprayed with a phytotoxic insecticide *with* added herbicide safener is tested, relative to plants sprayed with a phytotoxic insecticide *without* added safener.

Our experimental data reveals that for 20 sprayed plants, all 20 show phytotoxicity in the absence of the safener, while only 19 of those sprayed with the safener show phytotoxicity. Clearly, the one symptom-free plant could result from chance, and there would be no reason to reject the Null hypothesis.

If, however, 19 of the safener treated plants showed no sign of phytotoxicity, common sense would lead us to conclude that this was extremely unlikely to happen due to chance and we would reject the Null hypothesis, concluding that the treatment had an effect.

But what if only nine plants showed no sign of phytotoxicity - here, more than common sense is required to determine the likelihood of this occurring due to chance, and we will need to calculate the probability of the Null hypothesis being rejected - and that the safener treatment *does* have a significant effect.

A biological rule of thumb is that a 5% significance level is considered appropriate, meaning that we can be 95% confident that there is, in fact, a difference between treatments.

Stated in statistical terms, the typical significance level (alpha) of 0.05 (5%) corresponds to a 95% confidence level - we are 95% confident that we will not make a Type-I error (identifying false positives) and reject the Null hypothesis despite its being true.

In other words, only 5% of our experiments will give us a false positive. This level is termed the *"critical value"*. If the test statistic falls below the critical value (in this case $\alpha=0.05$), we accept the null hypothesis (H0), if it falls above the critical value, we reject the null hypothesis.

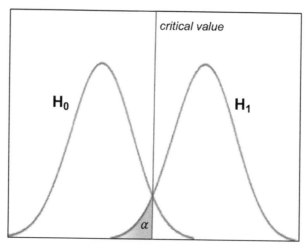

Figure 4.2: Significance level as determined by the critical value. If the test statistic falls below the critical value, we accept the null hypothesis (H0). α (alpha) represents the probability of making a Type-I error: rejecting our Null-hypothesis even though it is true (false positive).

The 5% significance level is a threshold arbitrarily decided on by biologists and is the threshold most commonly used in the Biological Sciences. Depending on the trial circumstances, *i.e.* what the data is to be used for, a 1% or 10% significance level may be appropriate.

Significance Rule of Thumb II: if the cost of a false positive is high (leading to a strategic decision to initiate a costly development process) thresholds for critical trials may be more stringent (1%). Conversely, if the cost of a false negative is high (leading to you missing out on a valuable discovery), the threshold for initial screening experiments may be raised to e.g. 10%.

If the cost of a false positive is high (for example leading to a strategic decision to initiate a costly development process) thresholds for critical trials may be made more stringent (1%).

Conversely, if the cost of a false negative is high (leading to you missing out on a valuable discovery), the threshold for initial screening experiments may be raised to, *e.g.* 10%.

If the probability (p-value, or "p") that the test statistic calculated from the observed data occurred by chance is less than $\alpha = (5\%)$, we may reject the Null hypothesis. This is commonly phrased as "a small p-value indicates that the Null hypothesis is not a good explanation for the data - we can be 95% confident that the alternative hypothesis is true".

This opens for one of the most hotly debated topics in biological statistics - the misuse of the p-value. Statisticians argue that it is incorrect to transpose the observation of a "5% chance of getting the observed results if the Null hypothesis is correct" into an observation of a "95% probability that the Null hypothesis is false" or "95% certainty that the observed difference is real and could not have arisen by chance" or "the difference is statistically significant".

It is beyond the scope of this book to expand on this debate[1] but suffice to say the above transposition is commonly used in the biological sciences, and the following paragraphs should be read with the above in mind.

It is common practice in most of the sciences to provide a p-value resulting from a statistical test and on this basis to conclude that the results are significant or not significant.

As seen above, the 5% significance level is a threshold arbitrarily decided on by biologists.

p-value	Graphical representation	Level of significance
<0.001	$***$	Very highly significant
<0.01	$**$	Highly significant
<0.05	$*$	Significant
<0.1		Approaching significance
0.1 or more		Not significant - more than 10% probability of chance

Figure 4.3: p-values and associated levels of "statistical significance".

Almost immediately, it appears, biologists (probably those that had p<0.06% datasets!) began to argue that fixed significance levels were too restrictive for biological data sets and devised a system of graduated levels of "the difference is statistically significant".

This tendency to correlate p-values with significance should be tempered with the consideration of whether the observed differences are substantively important.

For example, a small difference in efficacy between two treatments maybe statistically significant according to the above (hypothesis p-value) definition, but this difference may be too small to make it commercially meaningful (biologically significant).

For this reason, statisticians typically recommend estimating the effect size and evaluating confidence intervals for the differences between means, to emphasize the importance of the *magnitude* of the effect rather than merely statistically significant/non-significant hypothesis testing. These parameters will be discussed in the following.

Effect Size

Statisticians define *effect size* as the minimum acceptable deviation from the Null hypothesis and is a quantitative measure of the magnitude of the difference between the two groups, H0 and H1:

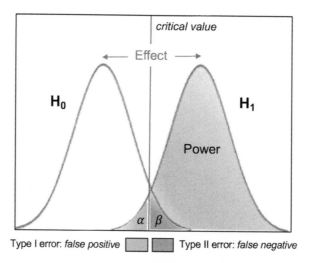

Figure 4.4: *Effect size is a measure of the magnitude of the difference between H0 and H1 and is often defined as the minimum improvement in efficacy needed to justify the costs of developing a new product.*

For crop protection researchers, effect size (or treatment effect) is often defined as the minimum improvement in efficacy needed to justify the costs of developing a new pesticide formulation.

A biological rule of thumb is that an effect size (treatment effect or improvement in efficacy) of 20% is considered economically viable.

As we will see shortly, effect size can have a significant influence on the number of replicates needed to perform the experiment. The trade-off is cost and space; it is not always feasible to include the requisite number of replicates in, for example, a greenhouse experiment.

Power or Sensitivity of a Test

The *power or sensitivity of a test* is used to determine the appropriate sample size for a test or experiment.

Before planning an experiment, researchers must consider which level of statistical power is sufficient to ensure that the test is sensitive enough to identify the difference between treatments.

Stated in statistical terms, *Power is the probability of correctly rejecting the Null hypothesis when it is false* and identifying a significant effect when such an effect exists.

The probability of Type II error is controlled by the power (sensitivity) of the test, denoted by beta (β), which is typically set at 0.10 or 0.20 (respectively a 90% (or 80%) chance of identifying a significant effect when such an effect exists.

A biological rule of thumb is that a Power of 80% is considered appropriate, meaning that there is only a 20% chance of erroneously concluding that there was no difference in efficacy between the treatments.

The trade-off is that the principal way to increase statistical power is to increase the number of replicates or the number of treatments - depending on the variability of biological material. This can require so many replicates that the trial becomes economically and practically unfeasible.

Researchers need to calculate the lowest sample sizes which will permit a statistically viable experiment.

To be able to do this, the statistical power of the test must be defined, and the *variability* or *variance* within the experimental setup must be determined.

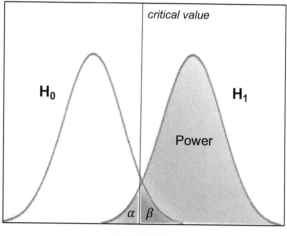

Type I error: *false positive* ▢ ▨ Type II error: *false negative*

Figure 4.5: Power (or sensitivity of a test) is the probability of correctly rejecting the Null hypothesis when it is false and identifying a significant effect when such an effect exists. α (alpha) represents the probability of making a Type-1 error: rejecting our Null-hypothesis even though it is true (false positive). β (beta) represents the probability of making a Type-II error: accepting our Null-hypothesis even though it is false (false negative).

Factors determining whether the test is sensitive enough to identify the difference between treatments, and to control the probability of Type I and Type II errors are summarized here:

Significance level: The significance level (alpha) is the probability of rejecting the null hypothesis when it is actually true. A lower significance level means that the test is more stringent and less likely to reject the null hypothesis, leading to lower power. Conversely, **a higher significance level means that the test is less stringent and more likely to reject the null hypothesis, leading to higher power.**

Variability: The variability in the data is the degree to which the observations or measurements differ from each other. **A higher variability generally leads to lower power because it makes it more difficult to detect a true effect or difference.** If the variability is large, the test may not be able to distinguish between the true effect and random variation, leading to lower power.

Effect size: The effect size is the magnitude of the difference or relationship between the groups or variables being compared. **A larger effect size generally leads to higher power because it makes the difference between the groups or variables easier to detect.** If the effect size is small, the test may not be able to detect the difference between the groups or variables, leading to lower power.

Sample size: The sample size is the number of observations or participants in a study. **A larger sample size generally leads to higher power** because it reduces the sampling error and increases the precision of the estimate. The larger the sample size, the more likely the test is to detect a true effect or difference, leading to higher power.

1. Although the p-value was introduced by Karl Pearson, it was extensively applied and disseminated in R.A. Fishers "Statistical methods for research workers" (1925). Here, he advocated the 5% significance level, (identifying that 1.96 standard deviations around the mean is the approximate value of the 97.5 percentile point of the normal distribution) which in turn led to the rule of thumb of two standard deviations for statistical significance in a normal distribution. One cannot help noticing the irony in light of the ongoing (often heated) debate regarding the use of p-values rather than fixed significance levels!

5

VARIANCE

An experiment comprises an independent as well as a dependent variable. The independent variable (in our example, the herbicide safener) can be changed or controlled (included or eliminated), and the effect it has on the dependent variable (insecticide phytotoxicity) can be recorded and analyzed.

A third group of variables are termed controlled variables and are those variables which the researcher controls (holds constant) and quantifies (records) during an experiment.

Temperature is a typical controlled variable - as temperature could affect the degree of phytotoxicity, it is important that it is held constant during the experiment. Other controlled variables relevant for biological trials include light, humidity and the variability within laboratory equipment.

Variance

Variance is the final factor which determines the required sample size (number of treatments or number of replicates) when designing an experiment. For the estimation of variance in a specific trial, the experimental standard deviation will need to be determined.

Variance is a measure of how far a data set is spread out or differs from the mean value. Variance is defined as the average of the squares of the differences between the observed values and the calculated average.

A biological data set will typically have a high variance, and experimental variance may arise from a number of sources including variance within the biological material being tested, researcher variance, equipment variance, and climatic variance.

Standard Deviation

Standard deviation (SD) is calculated as the square root of the variance, and approximates the average difference, or "spread" of the data set from the mean.

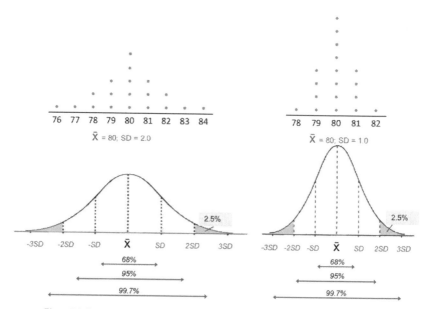

Figure 5.1: For an approximately Normal data set, the two-tailed values within one-, two- and three standard deviations of the mean account for about 68%, 95%; and 99.7% of the set, respectively.

Why bother calculating the square root of the variance? Simple – the standard deviation is expressed in the same units as the mean ($\bar{x}$), whereas variance is expressed in squared units. Standard deviation is thus a more intuitive method of indicating the spread of our data around the mean.

From figure 5.1, we can see that about 68%, 95% and 99.7% of the values in a Normal distribution lie within one, two and three standard deviations of the mean, respectively. For practical purposes, scientists assume that their data is derived from an approximately Normal data set.

One-tailed vs. two-tailed tests

In Figure 5.1, the standard deviation intervals are based on a two-tailed (or two-sided) test, which distributes the possibility of an effect in both directions: positive and negative.

Stated in other terms: a two-tailed test divides your significance level, and each direction is only half as "strong" as a one-tailed test, in which the significance level is applied in a single direction.

Without going into more detail, it is sufficient to know that for biological testing, two-sided tests should be used, unless there is reason (and you have the statistical insight) to do otherwise.

Two-sided Rule of Thumb: for the biological sciences, two-sided statistics should be used, unless there is reason (and you have the statistical insight) to do otherwise.

Normal distribution

Normal data distributions are symmetrical and follow a bell-shaped density curve (see Figure 5.1), with data distribution denser in the center (around the mean) and less dense in the tails.

Normality Rule of Thumb: for biological data, a Normal distribution may be assumed as a valid working approximation.

For biological data, the assumption of Normality is generally a valid approximation, as the Normal distribution of biological data is surprisingly ubiquitous. If the data is clearly not Normally distributed, it may need to be transformed - this will be discussed in a later chapter.

Estimating Standard Deviation

Standard deviation may be estimated from pilot trials or similar, prior experiments. Often as a researcher, you will be handed a set of data from a similar trial and expected to give an on the spot evaluation of its variance.

A useful trick to have up your sleeve is the ability to give a rough estimate of the standard deviation of a data set using the Range Rule of Thumb:

Range Rule of Thumb: SD ≈ Range/4 where Range = (maximum value) - (minimum value).

The Range Rule becomes more accurate when written as SD ≈ Range/SQRT(n). So, to be able to give a quick estimate of the standard deviation by glancing at a table of data, we may use the Range Rule for estimating Standard Deviation (SD):

SD ≈ Range/SQRT(n)	
SD estimate	**Dataset**
SD ≈ Range/2	<7
SD ≈ Range/3	8 - 12
SD ≈ Range/4	12 - 20

For rapid estimates of Standard Deviation in efficacy (0-100%) datasets, the following graphical representation provides a useful reference:

		Data set size (n)		
		<7	**8-12**	**12-20**
	60	30	20	15
	55	28	18	14
	50	25	17	13
	45	23	15	11
	40	20	13	10
Range	**35**	18	12	9
	30	15	10	8
	25	13	8	6
	20	10	7	5
	15	8	5	4
	10	5	3	3
	5	3	2	1

Figure 5.2: Standard Deviation estimates for selected ranges and data set sizes.

Let us consider our proposed experiment in which plants sprayed with a phytotoxic insecticide with added herbicide safener is to be tested, relative to plants sprayed with a phytotoxic insecticide without added safener.

In a previous pilot trial using the phytotoxic insecticide against the same plant species we intend to use, the results of 19 replicates were distributed as shown in Figure 5.1 (left).

The range is thus 84 - 76 = 8 and applying the Range rule of Thumb allows us to quickly estimate SD as 8/4 = 2. In this example, a calculation of SD gives the same result.

We will examine the usefulness of the standard deviation, Coefficient of Variation and effect size in more detail in the later section: *Descriptive Statistics - Critically evaluating experimental data.*

―――――

6

SAMPLE SIZE & REPLICATION

Replication is the repeated application of treatments to multiple independently assigned experimental units. The number of independently assigned experimental units that receive the same treatment is the sample size.

To obtain a rough estimate of the number of replicates required to generate a data set with a specific effect size, significance level and power, the estimated coefficient of variation for the experiment first needs to be determined:

Coefficient of Variation

Experimental variability may be expressed as the percent data spread relative to the mean and is termed the Coefficient of Variation or Coefficient of Variance (CoV), also known as the Relative Standard Deviation (RSD).

Calculation of the CoV should only be performed on data measured on the ratio scale (*e.g.*, mass, length, duration, disease severity, etc.), and on Normally distributed data (see previous chapter).

Also, it should be noted that when the mean value is small (approaching zero) the CoV may become extremely large and will be sensitive to small changes in the mean. Accordingly, CoV for *e.g.* crop protection trials are typically calculated for the ED50 (the dose giving a 50% effect).

The Coefficient of Variation may be calculated as:

$$CoV = (SD/MEAN)*100$$

The Coefficient of Variation describes the size of the standard deviation or data spread relative to the mean (or average). Standard Deviation and Mean may be estimated from pilot trials or similar, prior experiments.

Accordingly, in our proposed experiment in which plants sprayed with a phytotoxic insecticide with and without added herbicide safener is to be tested, the results of an initial pilot trial indicate that the data range was thus 84% efficacy (highest value) - 76% efficacy (lowest value) = 8 (see previous chapter).

Applying the Range rule of Thumb allows us to estimate SD as $8/4 = 2$. From this we may estimate the Coefficient of Variation as $CoV = (2/80)*100 = 2.5\%$

A biological rule of thumb is that a coefficient of variation of 20% or less is considered acceptable.

As variance increases for an experiment, it becomes more difficult to detect a significant difference, and a larger sample size will be required. In the absence of pilot trials or similar prior experiments, assumptions of CoV may be used together with Power and Effect Size (see earlier chapters) for a rough estimate of required sample size when designing experiments.

Biological assumptions for estimating number of replicates

- a variability (CoV) of 20% or less is considered acceptable.

- a $\alpha=5\%$ significance level is considered appropriate, meaning that only 5% of our experiments will give us a false positive. If the cost of a false positive is high, thresholds for critical trials may be made more stringent (1%). Conversely, if the cost of a false negative is high, the threshold for initial screening experiments may be raised to, e.g. 10%.

- an effect size (treatment effect or efficacy improvement) of 20% is considered economically viable (RRDI).

- a Power of 80% is considered appropriately sensitive, meaning that there is a 80% chance of identifying a significant effect when such an effect exists - the test is sensitive enough to identify the difference between treatments.

Assumptions for Design of Experiments (DOE)	
Significance (stringency)	5% (10)
Variability (CoV)	≤20%
Effect (difference)	20%
Power (sensitivity)	80% (90)

Figure 6.1: Assumptions for Design of Experiments (DOE).

With an indication of the relative data spread or variability, an estimate for the number of replicates required to achieve typical levels of significance, power and effect size may be obtained from the following tables, for a single sample (e.g. is it true that the treatment effect is greater than 0, the expected effect of an untreated control, UTC).

For comparing two treatments (e.g. treated and untreated control), the following table may be used to conveniently estimate the number of replicates needed based on CoV and Effect size, assuming 80% power and 5% significance:

Consider our proposed experiment in which plants sprayed with a phytotoxic insecticide with and without added herbicide safener is to be tested.

Development — α: 5%

% variability in Observations (CoV)	Effect Size 10	15	20	25	30
5	4	3	3	3	3
10	14	6	3	3	3
15	32	14	7	4	3
20	58	24	13	8	5
25	90	38	20	12	8
30	130	55	29	17	11
35	177	74	39	24	15
40	231	97	51	31	20

Discovery — α: 10%

% variability in Observations (CoV)	Effect Size 10	15	20	25	30
5	3	3	3	3	3
10	7	3	3	3	3
15	16	7	4	3	3
20	29	12	6	4	3
25	45	19	10	6	4
30	65	27	14	9	6
35	88	37	20	12	8
40	115	48	26	15	10

Figure 6.2: Sample sizes for a range of COV and effect sizes for comparing two treatments, two-sided and assuming 80% power and 5% significance (for Development trials) and 10% (for Discovery trials. Based on "Statistical Rules of Thumb" by Gerald van Belle (2008).

In the absence of any pilot trial data, or data from similar trials we may start with some underlying assumptions: a treatment effect of 20% (the safener-treated plants will need to show at least 20% less phytotoxicity to make further development worthwhile, and an assumption of 20% variability (CoV) is a realistic estimate of variability. We can now roughly estimate that each of the treatments will require 13 replicates (Figure 6.2).

For trials with a greater number of treatments or "experimental units", the number of replicates required may be determined from the **minimum accepted degrees of freedom for a biological trial**. This will be covered in the next chapter.

———

7

EXPERIMENTAL DEGREES OF FREEDOM

For trials with a greater number of treatments or "experimental units", the number of replicates required may be determined from the **minimum accepted degrees of freedom for a biological trial**.

Degrees of freedom refers to the number of independent pieces of information used to calculate the statistic. The degrees of freedom are calculated by subtracting one from the number of samples in your data set.

Simply put - for a one-sample statistical test, *i.e.* two treatments (one herbicide sample plus an untreated control), one degree of freedom is spent estimating the mean of the sample, while the remaining n-1 degrees of freedom are available to estimate variability.

When comparing two treatments, a larger number of replicates per treatment is required to achieve sufficient statistical power because the variability within each treatment needs to be estimated accurately.

This ensures that any observed differences between the two treatments are not due to random chance or natural variability. By increasing the number of replicates per treatment, the estimates of variability become more reliable, increasing the likelihood of detecting a true difference if it exists.

On the other hand, when comparing multiple treatments, the variability within each treatment is still important, but the focus shifts more towards capturing the overall variation between the treatments.

Since the variability between treatments tends to be larger than the variability within treatments, fewer replicates per treatment are needed to detect meaningful differences between the treatments.

This is because the increased variability between treatments provides more information for statistical analysis and increases the chances of detecting true differences.

The minimum accepted number of degrees of freedom required for a trial design to be considered adequate is 12 (*EPPO Guidelines, Design and analysis of efficacy evaluation trials - EPPO PP 1/152(4)*).

A biological rule of thumb is that the minimum accepted number of degrees of freedom required for a trial design is ≥12

However, this should be increased if there is low precision in the measurements taken, and for biological trials, a minimum residual degree of freedom of 15 is considered appropriate for a useful statistical analysis.

The EPPO Guidelines note that the actual number of degrees of freedom needed for a given trial may depend on various factors, including the expected variability of the response variable, the magnitude of treatment effects, and the desired level of statistical power.

Therefore, researchers are advised to carefully consider these factors when planning their trials and adjust the sample size accordingly to achieve an appropriate number of degrees of freedom.

The EPPO Guidelines do not explicitly provide specific values for the variability of the response variable, the size of treatment effects, or the desired level of statistical power that underlie the recommendation for a minimum of 10 degrees of freedom per treatment group.

However, if we extrapolate the data provided in the guidelines, it appears they are based on the *"Assumptions for Design of Experiments (DOE)"* presented in the previous chapter.

One-sample degrees of freedom

For an efficacy data set for one herbicide with ten replicates, the degrees of freedom will be:

10df (1 sample x 10 replicates) - 1 sample df = 9df

Here the degrees of freedom may be increased by increasing the replication. If this is not possible, degrees of freedom may be increased by increasing the number of treatments or the number of sites (replication of the experiment).

· · ·

Two-sample degrees of freedom

For a two-sample t-test, *i.e.* three treatments (two herbicide samples plus an untreated control) one degree of freedom is spent estimating each mean, while the remaining n-2 degrees of freedom are available to estimate variability.

If you are comparing the efficacy of two herbicides at comparable doses (*i.e.* 3 treatments: two herbicides plus the untreated control), with 10 replicates for each treatment, the degrees of freedom will be:

$$20df \ (2 \ samples \ x \ 10 \ replicates) - 2 \ sample \ df = 18df$$

Degrees of Freedom for a single, completely randomized site

Degrees of Freedom for a single, completely randomized site (*e.g.* a typical greenhouse trial) for selected combinations of Replicates and Treatments may conveniently be obtained from the following table (Figure 7.1).

From this table we can see that for a trial with 4 treatments (3 herbicide samples plus an untreated control) and 3 replicates, there are only 6 residual df. We will thus need at least 5 replicates to obtain df=12, while 6 replicates to obtain df=15 would be preferred.

					Replicates				
		3	4	5	6	7	8	9	10
	2	2	3	4	5	6	7	8	9
	3	4	6	8	10	12	14	16	18
	4	6	9	12	15	18	21	24	27
Treatments	5	8	12	16	20	24	28	32	36
	6	10	15	20	25	30	35	40	45
	7	12	18	24	30	36	42	48	54
	8	14	21	28	35	42	49	56	63
	9	16	24	32	40	48	56	64	72
	10	18	27	36	45	54	63	72	81

Figure 7.1: Degrees of freedom for replicates and treatment numbers, single site (5% significance).

Alternatively, we could repeat this trial at an additional site - doubling the df to 12, or (as is common for crop protection field trials) at three sites, tripling the degrees of freedom to 18.

From this table we can see that for a trial with 4 treatments (3 herbicide samples plus an untreated control) and 3 replicates, there are only 6 residual df. We will thus need at least 5 replicates to obtain df=12, while 6 replicates to obtain df=15 would be preferred.

Now that we have determined how large our trial needs to be (sample size; replicates), this would be an excellent time to head out into the greenhouse and consider how our trial is to be set up! Once we have identified the number of replicates to be used in our experiment, we may now consider how to assign and distribute (randomize) our experimental units.

———

8

RANDOMIZATION AND
EXPERIMENTAL DESIGN

One of British statistician and geneticist R.A. Fisher's (1892-1962) most important contributions to statistical methods is the introduction of randomization to experimentation, providing solutions to issues of variance arising from factors such as the heterogeneity of soils and the variability of biological material.

In biological trials, randomization is the process of randomly allocating experimental units (*e.g.* pots comprising treatments, references, untreated controls, as well as application timings and -doses) across the treatment groups.

Randomization provides a basis for the statistical methods used in generating and analyzing data by reducing bias, such as selection bias (our tendency to see patterns when evaluating experiments).

Controls

Scientific controls are part of the scientific method. Untreated controls are always included when designing experiments to confirm that observed effects are in fact due to the treatment. To control for confounding variables, such as the physical effects of spraying plants, untreated controls in crop protection trials are typically sprayed with water, or with a solution of formulation compounds from which the active ingredient has been eliminated.

For crop protection trials, the principal randomized designs in common use are the Completely Randomized Design (CRD) and the Randomized Complete Block Design (RCBD).

The Completely Randomized Design (CRD)

In a Completely Randomized Design (CRD) treatments are distributed at random. Each experimental unit (such as a plot of land or a group of plants) is randomly assigned to one of the treatment groups.

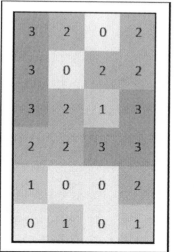
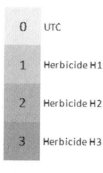

Figure 8.1: Completely Randomized Design (CRD) for four treatments (one untreated control, UTC and three herbicide samples).

This means that each experimental unit has an equal chance of receiving any particular treatment. CRD is relatively straightforward to implement, especially when the number of treatments is small and the experimental units are homogeneous.

Carried out on a greenhouse table, the pots could be randomly placed as shown in Figure 8.1. For a trial with four treatments (one untreated control, UTC and three herbicide samples, H1, H2 and H3), we can see from the previous section that we need six replicates to attain 15df.

The Randomized Complete Block Design (RCBD)

Completely Randomized Design (CRD) assumes that conditions across the greenhouse table (or field) are equivalent.

In reality this is rarely the case, and we can expect variation in temperature, light and humidity depending on the experimental units (pots) proximity to windows, insulated walls, etc.

These differences may be reduced by optimal greenhouse design, but their presence and influence on plant growth and response may also be addressed statistically by restricting the randomization process to form blocks.

The goal of blocking is to reduce the variability caused by factors that are not of primary interest in the study.

For example, if different sections of a field have different soil fertility levels, blocking can help ensure that each treatment is represented equally across those sections.

By incorporating blocking into the experimental design, RCBD provides more precise estimates of treatment effects and enhances the ability to detect smaller differences between treatments.

These blocks, containing all the treatments, treatment levels or combinations (called complete blocks) are typically set up at right angles to variance gradients.

In Figure 8.2, we take a temperature gradient (due to proximity to uninsulated glass panels and insulated interior walls) into account by placing blocks at right angles to the gradient.

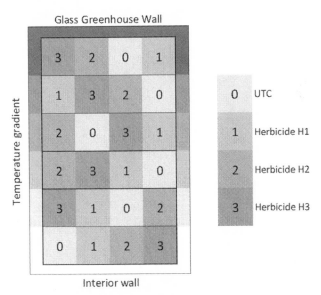

Figure 8.2: Randomized Complete Block Design (CRD) for four
treatments (one untreated control, UTC and three herbicide samples).

Each treatment appears in each (complete) block, and are assigned at random within the block, and for 6 replicates we have six blocks.

It is common practice in crop protection trials to ensure (for demonstration purposes) that a single block retains the treatment order as described in the experimental protocol.

RCBD enhances the ability to detect smaller differences between treatments, especially when there is a need to control specific factors. The Randomized Complete Block Design (RCBD) is more precise than the Completely Randomized Design (CRD) because it accounts for variability among experimental units by grouping them into blocks.

Each block contains a complete set of treatments, therefore differences among blocks are not due to treatments, and this variability can be estimated as a separate source of variation. The removal of an appreciable amount of this source of variation reduces experimental error and improves the ability of the experiment to detect smaller treatment differences.

Completely Randomized Design (CRD) is a design where each experimental unit (e.g. plot or a group of pot) is randomly assigned to one of the treatment groups, so each unit has an equal chance of receiving a specific treatment.

Randomized Complete Block Design (RCBD) incorporates blocking to reduce variability caused by factors not of primary interest, resulting in more precise treatment effect estimates when there is significant variability or a need to control specific factors.

In addition to Randomized Complete Block Design (RCBD) and Completely Randomized Design (CRD), there are several other options for randomization in experimental crop protection trials:

A **Latin square design** is used when there are two blocking factors. The treatments are arranged in a square such that each treatment occurs once in each row and column. This design is useful when you want to control for two sources of variability (such as temperature gradient and plant variety) that may affect the response variable.

In **split-plot designs**, when some factors are harder to vary than others at the level of experimental units, it is more efficient to assign the difficult-to-randomize factors (such as irrigation) to larger units (whole plots) and then apply the easier-to-randomize factor (pesticide treatment) to smaller units (subplots). Suppose you want to test the effect of irrigation amount and pesticide type on crop yield. Varying the level of irrigation is difficult on a small scale, so it makes more sense to apply irrigation levels to larger areas of land. You could divide each field into two large plots (whole plots) and apply irrigation amounts to each plot randomly. Then, divide each of these large plots into smaller plots (subplots) and apply pesticide randomly within the whole plots.

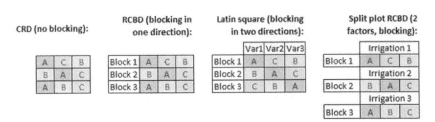

Figure 8.3: Overview of commonly used Randomization options.

These designs offer flexibility in accommodating specific experimental requirements and can enhance the precision and efficiency of crop protection trials by effectively managing various sources of variation.

Randomization offers researchers various approaches to manage sources of variation and increase the validity and precision of their results. By selecting an appropriate randomization method based on the specific characteristics and requirements of the study, researchers can ensure unbiased comparisons and draw robust conclusions about the efficacy of crop protection treatments.

With this information on Experimental Design, and the information on the Scientific Method and Hypotheses as well as Experimental Parameters presented in previous chapters - we are ready to initiate our experiment and move on to the next section: Descriptive Statistics - Critically evaluating experimental data.

———

III

DESCRIPTIVE STATISTICS - CRITICALLY EVALUATING EXPERIMENTAL DATA

9

DESCRIPTIVE STATISTICS: SD, SE OR 95%CI?

Once we have identified possible outliers (due to biological variance or experimental malfunction) and eliminated them as appropriate (see previous chapter), we are ready to continue the critical evaluation of our experimental data in the form of Descriptive Statistics.

Descriptive Statistics are used to describe the basic features of our experimental data and, together with graphical representations, can provide simple summaries about the Variability, Means, and Significance of our data.

The most common descriptive statistics used in the biological sciences are those of sample Standard Deviation (SD), Standard Error of the Mean (SEM) and 95% Confidence Intervals (95%CI).

Standard Deviation (SD)

Standard Deviation is used to quantify variability in the experimental data and is expressed in the same units as the data.

While calculators and spreadsheets can calculate Standard Deviation at the click of a button, it is occasionally useful to be able to give a rough estimate of the Standard Deviation of a data set using the **Range Rule of Thumb:**

SD ≈ Range/SQRT(n)	
SD estimate	Dataset
SD ≈ Range/2	<7
SD ≈ Range/3	8 - 12
SD ≈ Range/4	12 - 20

Figure 9.1: Range Rule of Thumb to estimate the Standard Deviation of a data set.

This rule of thumb provides a useful estimation for samples sizes greater than n=12. For many biological trials, sample sizes are smaller, and division by 3 (for n = 8-12) or 2 (for n < 7) provides a better estimate (see earlier chapter).

Standard deviation (SD) is calculated as the square root of the variance, and approximates the average difference, or "spread" of the data set from the mean. By squaring the variance the standard deviation is expressed in the same units as the mean. Standard deviation is thus a more intuitive method of indicating the spread of our data around the mean.

Population standard deviation and sample standard deviation are both measures of how spread out a set of data is, but they are calculated differently and are used to describe different groups of data.

The difference between the population and the sample standard deviation is that when calculating the sample standard deviation, we divided by n-1 instead of n to correct the tendency to underestimate the true variability in the population.

Population standard deviation is the measure of how much the data points in an entire population deviate from the population mean. Sample standard deviation, on the other hand, is the measure of how much the data points in a subset, or sample, of the population deviate from the sample mean.

For crop protection trials, we may wish to calculate the standard deviation of the height of ten plants in a treatment. Here we should use the population standard deviation, as we are only interested in the heights of the ten plants in our treatment, and not the plants in any other treatment.

The Standard Deviation cannot be used to determine whether the difference between Means is significant and can only be used to express variability, or to derive the Standard Error of the Mean or its extension, the 95% Confidence Interval.

An example of a practical application of quantifying variability in a trial is given in figure 9.2, where it is apparent that the variability is different for each data point.

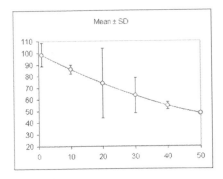

Figure 9.2: Differences in trial variability, expressed as Mean ± SD.

Accordingly, we can deduce that some independent factor (variance within the biological material being tested, researcher variance, equipment variance or climatic variance) contributed to variability and that we should return to our experimental setup to identify and remove this disturbance.

If you do not address this yourself, a reviewer will almost certainly insist that this experiment is repeated, leading to a significant delay in the publication of *e.g.* a scientific article.

Coefficient of Variance (CoV)

We saw in the previous section that as variance increases for an experiment, it becomes more difficult to detect a significant difference, and a larger sample size will be required. We learnt that Experimental variability may be expressed as the percent data spread relative to the mean (the signal:noise ratio) and is termed the Coefficient of Variation or Coefficient of Variance (CoV), also known as the Relative Standard Deviation (RSD).

$$CoV = (SD/MEAN)*100$$

From the perspective of critically evaluating experimental data, we have the:

Variability Rule of Thumb: a coefficient of variation of 20% or less is considered acceptable.

Before initiating a trial, the COV for the specific trial type should be determined, and the trial should only commence if the COV is considered acceptable. On critical evaluation of the trial data, it should be determined whether the data conforms to the agreed COV.

Evaluating Homogeneity of Variance

For two datasets, the **F-test** (next section) can be used to compare the variability of samples, to determine whether they have equal or different variances.

If you have access to a statistical package, you can use **Bartlett's test or Levene's test** to assess the equality of variances across multiple groups or samples.

Bartlett's test performs well with larger sample sizes, and is more sensitive to deviations from normality, while Levene's test is suitable for both small and large sample sizes and is less sensitive and more robust in the presence of non-normality.

Alternatively, you can critically evaluate your data by comparing the variability of samples using the **Homogeneity of Variances Rule of Thumb**: if the largest variance is no more than 4 times the small variance (i.e., if the largest standard deviation is less than two times the smallest standard deviation), you can assume the variance in each group is the same. With experience, you will be able to "eyeball" this difference.

Homogeneity of Variances Rule of Thumb: if the largest standard deviation is less than two times the smallest standard deviation, the variance in each group is probably equal.

In the following example, four treatments are evaluated as the effect of the treatment on the height of plants.

Using the calculated standard deviations and the Homogeneity of Variances rule of thumb, we see the largest standard deviation is greater than two times the smallest standard deviation, and can conclude that the variances are probably unequal.

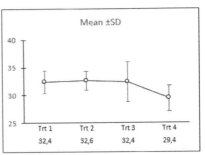

	Trt 1	Trt 2	Trt 3	Trt 4
	29	30	29	27
	34	32	30	28
	33	33	31	29
	34	34	34	33
	32	34	38	30
mean	32,4	32,6	32,4	29,4
SD	2,07	1,67	3,65	2,30

Homogeneity of variances - rule of thumb:		
SD -greater	3,65
SD - lesser	1,67
Ratio	2,18
Variances are:	**Unequal**

Figure 9.3: Comparing treatment variability using the Homogeneity of Variances Rule of Thumb.

Standard Error of the Mean (SE or SEM)

Standard Error of the Mean is derived from the Standard Deviation and quantifies the precision of the calculated Mean relative to the true population Mean, and considers the variability (Standard Deviation, SD) and the sample size (n) - factors which determine how close the sample Mean will be relative to the population Mean.

As for Standard Deviation, Standard Error of the Mean is expressed in the same units as the data, and is calculated as the Standard Deviation divided by the square root of the sample size:

$$SE = SD / SQRT(n)$$

It can be seen from the above equation that the Standard Error is always smaller than the Standard Deviation of a dataset and, in contrast to the Standard Deviation, the Standard Error always gets smaller as your sample size gets larger.

For this reason, Standard Error of the Mean is sometimes misused for data description, and it is generally recommended that 95% Confidence Intervals be used instead.

The 95% Confidence Interval (95% CI)

The 95% Confidence Interval is derived from the Standard Error of the Mean and quantifies the precision of the calculated Mean, such that the Confidence Interval contains the true population Mean with 95% certainty.

The 95% Confidence Interval of a Mean is calculated as the Standard Error of the Mean multiplied by a constant from the t-distribution for the given sample size (n-1 degrees of freedom, DF):

$$95\% CI = SEM * t(n-1)$$

While 95% Confidence intervals are easily calculated, it is occasionally useful to be able to give a rough estimate of these Intervals using the Confidence Interval Rule of Thumb:

Confidence Interval Rule of Thumb I: for large sample sizes, 95% Confidence Interval may be estimated from the Mean plus or minus two Standard Errors of the Mean.

The above is valid for large sample sizes, for smaller sample sizes the t-distribution provides a correction factor.

Referring to the t-distribution (Figure 9.4) we can see that t-values are close to two for datasets greater than twenty while for datasets less than 10 the t-value increases rapidly.

df	p= .05 2-tailed	df	p= .05 2-tailed
1	12.71	13	2.16
2	4.30	14	2.14
3	3.18	15	2.13
4	2.78	16	2.12
5	2.57	17	2.11
6	2.45	18	2.10
7	2.36	19	2.09
8	2.31	20	2.09
9	2.26	30	2.04
10	2.23	50	2.01
11	2.20	100	1.98
12	2.18	∞	1.96

Figure 9.4: t-distributions for given sample sizes (n-1 degrees of freedom, DF) for the calculation of 95% Confidence Intervals.

Plotting and interpreting SD, SEM and 95%CI Error bars

When plotting data with Error bars or creating tables with +/- values, SD, SEM, and 95%CI are often applied and interpreted incorrectly. Almost as frequently, Error bars are presented without any mention of what they indicate.

Let us begin by calculating the Mean Standard Deviation, Standard Error of the Mean and 95% Confidence Interval of a set of data. In the following example (Figure 9.5), the Mean is illustrated by use of a bar graph, to which the respective Error bars are added.

As we can see, the Standard Deviation Error bars are broader (further from the Mean) than those of the Standard Error of the Mean.

This is because the Standard Error of the Mean is calculated as the Standard Deviation divided by the square root of the sample size.

For this reason, Standard Errors of the Mean are sometimes presented as Error bars without any indication of their identity, with the intent of making variability seem as small as possible.

Even worse, this practice may mislead those who erroneously interpret non-overlapping Error bars as indicative of significant differences between the Means.

Standard Deviations should only ever be used to express the variation in our data and showing the variation in our data as a scatter plot usually provides more information then expressing the variation as Standard Deviation Error bars.

Standard Error of the Mean (SEM) Error bars may be used to express how accurately your data define the Mean, but if your objective is to compare Means, 95% Confidence Interval Error bars are more useful.

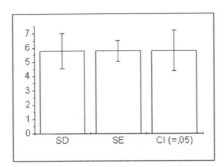

Figure 9.5: Bar graph for the Mean of a dataset showing Error bars for Standard Deviation (SD), Standard Error of the Mean (SE) and 95% Confidence Interval (CI), respectively.

In addition, Confidence Intervals may be used to provide an initial estimate of statistical significance, and Confidence Intervals are often easier to interpret than statements about statistical significance.

As an initial indication, if Confidence Intervals do NOT overlap, the Means are probably significantly different (at the $p < 0.05$ level). This may be confirmed as required using a valid statistical test (*e.g.* a two-sample t-test).

Confidence Interval Rule of Thumb II: if Confidence Interval Error bars do not overlap, the differences between the Means are probably significant; if Confidence Interval Error bars overlap by more than 25%, the differences between the Means are probably not significant.

It is important to be aware that the opposite is not necessarily true (a mistake made by students and scientists alike): if Confidence Intervals DO overlap, there may be a statistically significant difference between the Means, and it is thus NOT possible to deduce that the difference between the Means is NOT significant.

However, a statistical rule of thumb states that if Confidence Interval Error bars overlap by more than 25%, the Means are probably not significantly different at the $p < 0.05$ level) - to confirm this one should conduct a two-sample t-test and calculate the p-value.

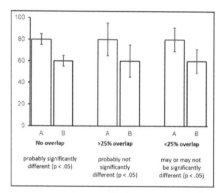

Figure 9.6: *Use of 95% Confidence Interval (95% CI) Error bars to estimate the significance of differences between Means.*

In conclusion: when used correctly, Standard Deviation, Standard Error of the Mean and 95% Confidence Intervals are useful descriptive statistics allowing us to critically evaluate our experimental data for variability (SD), proximity of the calculated Mean to the population Mean (SE) and may be used as a visual estimate of whether the differences between Means are significant (95%CI).

The principal advantage (and potential disadvantage) of using 95% Confidence Intervals to estimate the significance of differences between Means is that these calculations may be easily performed and interpreted without access to - or an understanding of - advanced statistical techniques.

———

10

IDENTIFICATION OF OUTLIERS: Q-TEST, IQR AND SD

In one of the first chapters, we began with the observation that a herbicide safener might reduce insecticide phytotoxicity, from which a research hypothesis was formulated.

To experimentally test the hypothesis we used significance levels, power, and effect to design a randomized complete block experiment in which plants were treated with insecticides in the absence or presence of safeners and evaluated for differences in phytotoxicity between treatments.

The experimental parameters were defined under the assumption that our data would be derived from an approximately normal data set.

We learned that for biological data, the assumption of normality is generally a valid approximation, as the normal distribution of biological data is surprisingly ubiquitous.

With the results of our evaluation in hand, the next step is to critically evaluate the experimental data by identifying and possibly rejecting outliers. Before proceeding, we should ensure that all values are correctly entered, and correct if necessary.

We then take experimental problems into account - if an apparent outlier derives from an experimental mistake or malfunction, it may be justified to exclude the value without performing additional calculations.

It should be noted that in addition to detecting outliers with the intention of eliminating them from subsequent statistical analyses, there is also the option of detecting outliers to identify datasets that qualify for retesting, or to identify outliers with the intention of retaining them for analysis using so-called robust statistical techniques.

The need to identify and remove outliers is reduced when the data is to be analyzed using "robust" methods of statistical analysis, such as nonparametric tests which compare the distribution of ranks.

Here the largest value will have the highest rank irrespective of how large that value is. If the data is to be statistically analyzed using parametric tests (which assume a Gaussian distribution, or Normalcy) the need to eliminate outliers is far greater.

Q-test for Outliers

The simplest method to identifying outliers in smaller datasets (n = 3-10) typical for biological trials is to use the Q-test published in 1951 by Robert Dean and Wilfred Dixon, for which we again assume Normalcy of our data (the Q-test prescribes that the data - excluding the possible outlier - must be Normally distributed).

We begin by arranging the data in order of increasing value and calculate Q as the Gap divided by the Range, where the Gap is the difference between the outlier and the closest number to it and the Range is the difference between the lowest and the highest value.

$$Q = GAP / RANGE$$

The null hypothesis for the Q-test is: there are no outliers in the dataset. If the value of Q is higher than the associated table value corresponding to the sample size and Confidence level (typically the 95% Confidence level, alpha = 0.05), the outlier may be rejected.

In the following experimental dataset, we wish to determine whether the value 77 is an outlier at the 95% Confidence level:

		84 85	
77	82	84 85 86 87	
.....GAP......			
	....................RANGE.........		

After sorting the data into ascending order, we can use the following formula to calculate the Q statistic by dividing the gap (5) by the range (10):

$$Q = GAP / RANGE = 5 / 10 = 0.5$$

From the schematized table of critical values for Q (below) we can quickly determine that our calculated Q statistic of 0.5 is less than the critical two-sided (*i.e.* determining for outliers at both extremes of the dataset) table value of 0.53 for a sample size of 8 at the most commonly used 95% Confidence level, and the data value 77 may thus NOT be rejected:

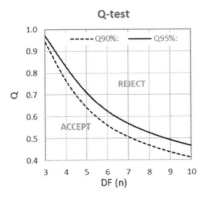

Figure 10.1: Outliers - schematized two-sided table for critical values of Q for 90% and 95% Confidence levels.

From the schematized table of critical values for Q (above) we can determine that our calculated Q statistic of 0.5 is less than the critical two-sided (*i.e.* determining for outliers at both extremes of the dataset) table value of 0.53 for a sample size of 8 at the most commonly used 95% Confidence level, and the data value 77 may thus NOT be rejected.

The Q-test for outliers is a mathematically simple procedure but does require that we take the time to consider the results logically: for example, performing the Q-test on the values 82.24; 82.25 and 82.25 returns the conclusion that 82.24 is an outlier! Clearly, statistical significance does not always equal practical significance.

An alternative method in common use for larger datasets is Grubb's test for outliers, in which outliers are identified as the difference between the outlier and the Mean, divided by the Standard Deviation. This ratio is then compared to a table of critical values.

The advantage of the Q-test relative to Grubb's test is that calculations may easily be made by hand, the disadvantage is that it is only valid for data sets up to n=10. However, for most experimental biological applications the Q-test is both appropriate and convenient.

· · ·

Interquartile Range (IQR) Test for Outliers

Box plots are a useful tool for identifying outliers in a dataset. Outliers are data points that are significantly different from the rest of the data and can skew the results of statistical analyses. Box plots display the distribution of data in a way that makes it easy to identify outliers.

The box in the plot represents the interquartile range (IQR), which is the range between the first and third quartiles. Any data points that fall outside of the whiskers of the box plot are considered outliers. The whiskers extend to the minimum and maximum values of the data, but any data points beyond 1.5 times the IQR from the edge of the box are considered outliers and are plotted as individual points.

The Interquartile Range (IQR) is a statistical measure that helps identify outliers in a dataset. It is determined by the range between the first quartile (Q1) and the third quartile (Q3) of the data.

To use the IQR for outlier identification, we calculate Q1 and Q3 and then find the range of values that lie within 1.5 times the IQR below Q1 or above Q3. Any data point that falls outside this range is considered a potential outlier.

Let's consider an example with two herbicide treatments. The mean height for treatment 1 is 70cm, and the mean height for treatment 2 is 38cm.

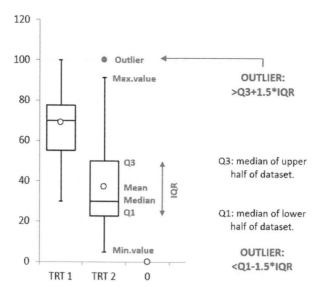

Figure 10.2: The Interquartile Range (IQR) to identify outliers in a dataset.

To determine outliers using the IQR, we start by creating a box plot. The box plot displays the distribution of data, with a box representing the IQR (the range between the first quartile, Q1 and the third quartile, Q3).

A line inside the box indicating the median, a circle to show the mean and "whiskers" extending from the box to show the range of non-outlier values (the range of values that lie within 1.5 times the IQR below Q1 or above Q3). Any data points beyond the whiskers are considered potential outliers.

By observing the box plot, we see that the value of 100cm in treatment 2 falls outside the whisker range, indicating it as a potential outlier.

SD Test for Outliers

An even simpler (but less accepted) method to detect and eliminate outliers is by using the standard deviation of the data distribution.

We may assume a value to be an outlier if it is more than 2 or 3 times the standard deviation of the distribution.

This method is based on the Rule of Thumb for Normal Distribution: The approximate percentage of values falling within one, two, and three standard deviations of the mean in a normal distribution is 68%, 95%, and 99.7%, respectively.

Data presentation for researchers and decision makers

For **researchers** evaluating the data, the box plot is a valuable tool to gain insights into the quality of the data and identify important characteristics. The box plot provides a visual summary of the data distribution, displaying the median, quartiles, and potential outliers.

By examining a **box plot**, researchers can quickly assess measures like skewness (indicating a departure from symmetry) and identify any outliers that might be influential or require further investigation. This helps researchers understand the overall pattern and variability in the data, aiding in data interpretation and potential adjustments to analysis methods.

When presenting data to **decision-makers** who may not have a statistical background, using a bar chart with error bars can be a helpful visual tool.

This type of chart shows the means of different groups or treatments, along with the 95% Confidence Interval (CI) represented by the error bars. The CI provides a range of values around the mean that we are reasonably confident the true population mean falls within.

Decision-makers often assume that if the error bars of two groups or treatments do not overlap, then the means are significantly different. While this assumption is not always accurate, the CI at least gives decision-makers a probability of making the right decision based on the available data. It's important to note that statistical significance should be properly tested using appropriate hypothesis tests (next section) rather than relying solely on visual cues.

Box plot for data evaluation:

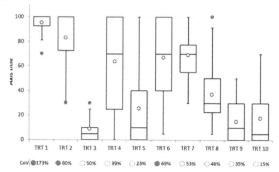

Bar graph ±95CI for presentation: Average ±95%CI

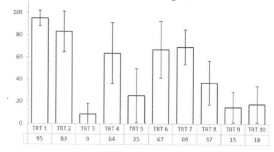

Figure 10.3: Data presentation for researchers and decision makers

By using **bar charts with 95% CI error bars** when presenting data to decision-makers and box plots during data evaluation, both parties can gain valuable insights.

Decision-makers obtain an understanding of potential differences between means based on the visual cues, while researchers can examine the data's characteristics more thoroughly and identify outliers or other important features that may impact the statistical analysis.

Ultimately, the combined use of these two visual tools enhances both the communication of findings and the researcher's ability to draw meaningful conclusions from the data.

———

11

CHI-SQUARE TEST: GOODNESS OF FIT FOR SAMPLE VALIDATION

The chi-squared distribution or $\chi2$-distribution, developed by English mathematician and statistician Karl Pearson in 1900 is a widely used probability distribution in inferential statistics (Section IV) and is a component of the t-distribution, f-distribution, the Analysis of Variance (Chapter 17) and regression analysis (Section V).

Chi-squared tests for the goodness-of-fit (within-sample deviations)

The chi-squared distribution is also used in chi-squared tests for the goodness of fit of an observed distribution - a component of experimental validation - by comparing expected and observed values.

In a typical validation study example, a within-sample comparison for individual observed values of bacterial counts on Petri dishes against average observed values is required to conform to an acceptance criterium, for example, within-sample deviation of $\chi2$ must conform to $p>0.05$ (see example below).

If the chi-square test indicates that the test result exceeds the stipulated criteria limit (we speak of the chi-square test failing to support the Null hypothesis: there is no difference between the counts) possible outliers may be removed from the evaluation.

No more than 20% of the counts (one in five) may be removed. If the Chi-square test fails after the removal of possible outliers - *i.e.* if p<0.05 - the sample is considered invalid and must be rejected.

In the following example, bacterial counts of a microbial biopesticide are performed on five Petri dishes. The Null hypothesis is that there is no difference between the observed counts (O), relative to the average (and thus expected, E) count:

Plate	1	2	3	4	5
Count (O)	60	61	66	60	66
Average (E)	62.6				
(O-E)^2/E	0.11	0.04	0.18	0.11	0.18
Σ(O-E)^2/E	0.63				

The deviation for each count relative to the average (E) is calculated as:

$$(O-E)^2/E$$

...while the $\chi 2$ value (the sum of deviations for each count relative to the average (E) is calculated as:

$$\chi 2 = \Sigma(O-E)^2/E$$

The calculated probability (P; $\chi 2$) - the likelihood that the within-sample deviation between expected (E) and observed (O) counts is due to chance - can be compared to the table values in Figure 11.1 for $n-1$ degrees of freedom (df).

If the $\chi 2$ probability lies above the 5% significance curve (p<0.05; Figure 11.1) the probability that the deviations are due to chance are small - the sample is considered invalid and must be rejected.

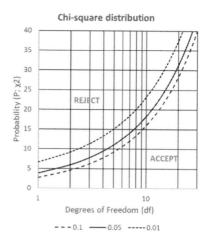

Figure 11.1: $\chi 2$ distributions for 2-20df; for 1%, 5% and 10% significance.

Conversely, if the χ2 probability falls below the 5% significance curve (p>0.05) the probability that the deviations are due to chance is great - the sample conforms to the acceptance criteria and can be accepted.

For our example, the calculated within-sample comparison values for individual observed counts against average observed counts ($\chi2=0.63$) are less than the critical value of 9.49 for 4df at 5% significance (Figure 11.1) and the sample thus conforms to the acceptance criteria and can be accepted.

———

12

CORRECTED EFFICACY FOR UNTREATED CONTROL MORTALITY

When evaluating the efficacy of insecticides, the assumption is made that the observed responses are due to the treatments only. However, in some cases the responses may occur independently of the treatments at zero dose (untreated control), for example through death of the untreated targets from natural causes.

In such cases it is possible to compensate for this by calculating corrected efficacy.

If the control mortality is above 20%, the results must be discarded. When control mortality is greater than 5% but less than 20%, the observed mortality must be corrected using the appropriate formula. If the control mortality is below 5%, it can be ignored, and no correction is necessary.

Corrected efficacy is a statistical approach that helps researchers accurately assess the effectiveness of a pesticide or treatment. By subtracting the control mortality from the treatment mortality, we isolate the mortality directly caused by the treatment.

This allows us to focus on the treatment effect specifically, separate from other factors. The purpose is to eliminate confounding factors and determine the true impact of the treatment in controlling pests or diseases.

Corrected efficacy can be calculated by appropriate methods, depending on whether the population is uniform (if there were no significant differences between the means in ANOVA *before* the treatment) or non-uniform, and whether the observation is based on infestation (live individuals) or mortality (dead individuals).

Uniform pest or disease infestation before treatment i.e., no significant differences between the means (ANOVA) - correction for natural mortality in untreated control plots

Non-uniform pest or disease infestation before treatment i.e., significant differences between the means (ANOVA) - correction for natural mortality and non-uniformity of infestation in untreated control plots

---

Abbott's method, Henderson-Tilton's method, Schneider-Orelli's method, and Sun-Shepard's method are all statistical approaches commonly used in agricultural and biological research to analyze and compare pesticide or treatment effects on pests or diseases. Here is a brief overview of each method:

Methods for corrected efficacy for infestation (live counts) data:

Abbott's method: Calculates efficacy based on treatment mortality as a percentage of the untreated control (Uniform pest or disease infestation before treatment).

Henderson-Tilton's method: Calculates efficacy based on change in infestation before and after treatment. It accounts for the natural or background mortality observed in the control group and allows for a more accurate estimation of the mortality caused by the pesticide treatment (Non-uniform pest or disease infestation before treatment).

Uniform disease or pest infestation before treatment	Abbott's method: $Corrected\ \% = (1 - \dfrac{Population\ in\ treated\ plot\ after\ treatment}{Population\ in\ control\ plot\ after\ treatment}) * 100$
Non-uniform disease or pest infestation before treatment	Henderson-Tilton's method: $Corrected\ \% = (1 - \dfrac{n\ in\ Co\ before\ treatment * n\ in\ T\ after\ treatment}{n\ in\ Co\ after\ treatment * n\ in\ T\ before\ treatment}) * 100$

Figure 12.1 : Abbot's method (uniform infestation) and Henderson-Tilton's method (non-uniform infestation) for corrected efficacy, infestation (alive)

84

Methods for corrected efficacy for mortality evaluation:

Schneider-Orelli's method: Calculates efficacy based on treatment mortality as a percentage of the untreated control (Uniform pest or disease infestation before treatment).

Sun-Shepard's method: Calculates efficacy based on change in control mortality before and after treatment (Non-uniform pest or disease infestation before treatment).

Uniform disease or pest infestation before treatment	**Schneider-Orelli's method:** $Corrected\ \% = (\dfrac{\%\ mortality\ in\ T - \%\ mortality\ in\ Co}{100 - \%\ mortality\ in\ Co}) * 100$
Non-uniform disease or pest infestation before treatment	**Sun-Shepard's method:** $Corrected\ \% = (\dfrac{\%\ mortality\ in\ T - \%\ change\ in\ Co}{100 - \%\ change\ in\ Co}) * 100$ $\%\ change\ in\ Co = \dfrac{n\ in\ Co\ after\ treatment - n\ in\ Co\ before\ treatment}{n\ in\ Co\ before\ treatment} * 100$

Figure 12.2: Schneider-Orelli's method (uniform infestation) and Sun-Shepard's method (non-uniform infestation) for corrected efficacy, mortality.

These methods may be simplified and summarized as follows:

	Uniform population	Non-uniform population
Infestation (live)	Abbot's % correction: $1 - \dfrac{nTa}{nCa} * 100$	Henderson-Tilton % correction: $1 - \dfrac{nCb * nTa}{nCa * nTb} * 100$
Mortality (dead)	Scheider-Orelli % correction: $1 - \dfrac{m\%T - m\%C}{100 - m\%C} * 100$	Sun-Shepard % correction: $1 - \dfrac{m\%T - \Delta\%C}{100 - \Delta\%C} * 100$

nT(C)a = number of insects in Treatment (Control) after treatment, and nT(C)b = number of insects in Treatment (Control) before treatment

m%T(C) = mortality % in Treatment (Control) and Δ%C = change % in Control.

Figure 12.3: Summary of methods for calculating corrected efficacy.

The following examples from crop protection trials show how the formulas translate into actual calculations and interpretations.

	Uniform population	Non-uniform population
Infestation (live)	Example: Abbot % correction In an experimental plot, 40 insects are observed in the control plot while only 30 insects were observed in the treated plot. The corrected efficacy is calculated as: $Corrected\ \% = \left(1 - \frac{30}{40}\right) * 100 = 25\%$	Example: Henderson-Tilton % correction After treatment, 40 insects are observed in the control vs only 30 insects in the treated plot, but 8 and 6 insects respectively were found before treatment: $Corrected\ \% = 1 - \frac{8 \cdot 30}{40 \cdot 6} * 100 = 0\%$
Mortality (dead)	Example: Scheider-Orelli % correction In an experimental plot, 10% mortality is observed in the control plot while 50% mortality is observed after treatment. The corrected efficacy is calculated as: $Corrected\ \% = \left(\frac{50-10}{100-10}\right) * 100 = 44\%$	Example: Sun-Shepard % correction In an experimental plot, a 25% change in mortality (from 8 to 10%) is observed in the control plot while 50% mortality is observed after treatment. The corrected efficacy is: $Corrected\ \% = \left(\frac{50-25}{100-25}\right) * 100 = 33\%$

Figure 12.4: Examples, corrected efficacy calculations.

———

IV

INFERENTIAL STATISTICS - ACCEPTING OR REJECTING THE HYPOTHESIS

13

DATA SCALES (DATA TYPES)

In the previous chapters, *Descriptive statistics* were shown to provide a summary of our dependent variable data in the form of measures of central tendency (mean) and measures of variability (variance, standard deviation, standard error of the mean, 95% confidence intervals, etc.).

In contrast to Descriptive statistics on sample data, *Inferential statistics* move beyond the immediate data to infer the significance of observed differences between treatments, and thus whether our data allows us to reject the null hypothesis.

Hypothesis testing

Hypothesis testing is a means of drawing conclusions about a population mean, and a range of tests are available to determine whether a hypothesis about the mean is true or not.

The choice of test is determined by the scale (type) and distribution of the data. The following section provides a brief overview of data scales or types.

Types of Data

Most experimental biological data are in the form of *measurement data,* or data expressed using an interval or ratio scale. The following provides a brief hierarchical overview of the four principal data scales, or types.

• • •

Nominal and Ordinal data

Nominal (non-numeric) and Ordinal (categorical numeric) data are rarely encountered in biological testing and comprise categorical or discrete variables and are typically described by two or more values (categories). Due to their non-numeric nature, it is possible to differentiate, but not to order or rank Nominal (such as "male" / "female") data.

Category	Type	Data	Description	Power	Variable	Descriptive statistics	Inferential statistics
Measurement	Numerical	Discrete or continuous	Amount of Difference; absolut zero	Increasing information	RATIO	Mean, SD, SEM, 95%CI	Parametric or non-parametric
			Amount of Difference		INTERVAL	Median, Min /Max, Range	
Rank / Count	Categorical	Discrete	Direction of Difference		ORDINAL	Mode, Counts, Frequency	Non-parametric
			Difference		NOMINAL		

Figure 13.1: Hierarchy of dependent variable data scales (types) and descriptions, including a summary of appropriate descriptive and inferential statistical analysis methods.

In contrast, it is possible to rank Ordinal data (such as shortest to tallest plant), providing an additional aspect of direction to the simple binary differentiation of Nominal data.

However, ordinal data categories do not have an equivalent distance between them, so a relative magnitude of the difference cannot be determined.

Nominal and Ordinal data may be summarized using descriptive statistics (mode, count, frequency) and hypotheses may be tested using *nonparametric* inferential statistics which do not assume a Normal or Gaussian distribution (see next chapter).

As Nominal and Ordinal data do not indicate the magnitude of the difference, they are referred to as *rank* or *count data*.

Interval and Ratio data

In contrast to Nominal and Ordinal data, Interval and Ratio data allow us to determine the magnitude of the difference and are thus referred to as measurement data.

Interval and Ratio data comprise continuous (as opposed to discrete) numeric variables and may contain any value with a finite or infinite interval, such as plant height, insect mass, disease incidence or -severity.

Data on an Interval scale do not contain a true zero (for example, temperature measured in degrees Centigrade or Fahrenheit), while data on the Ratio scale (such as weight or height) provide a true or absolute zero, from which we, for example, may determine that a treated plant is double as tall as an untreated control plant.

Interval and ratio data may be summarized using descriptive statistics (median, minimum/maximum, range) for interval data, or (mean, standard deviation, standard error of the mean and 95% confidence interval) for both interval and ratio data.

Hypotheses may be tested using *parametric* inferential statistics (which assume a Normal or Gaussian distribution) - the topic of the next chapter.

———

14

NONPARAMETRIC OR PARAMETRIC STATISTICAL TESTS

Inferential statistics enable us to test a hypothesis and draw conclusions, or inferences regarding a population through extrapolation from our experimental data sample.

Our choice of statistical method for hypothesis testing is based on whether the experimental data is normally distributed, and on the scale of the data.

Assumption of Normal (Gaussian) distribution

Parametric tests such as the *t*-test and ANOVA are generally more powerful than non-parametric tests and are more likely to detect a significant effect when one indeed exists. They assume that the samples follow a normal (Gaussian) distribution. A number of tests of normality are available, such as the **Shapiro–Wilk and Kolmogorov–Smirnov tests**, but these require statistical insight or access to statistical software packages.

A simpler graphical approximation to evaluate normality is to visually determine how closely a histogram of the sample resembles a "bell-shaped" normal probability curve (Figure 14.1).

If the shape of the histogram looks approximately symmetrical and bell-shaped, the assumption of normalcy can be considered reasonably met. A box plot (inset, Figure 14.1) also provides an overview of data distribution and can identify non-normal distributions.

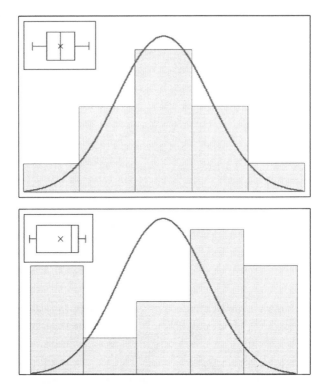

Figure 14.1: Histograms of sample data overlaid with a normal probability curve and box-plot (inset) identifying normal (top) and non-normal (bottom) data distributions.

A general rule of thumb is that the distribution of the mean approaches a normal distribution as sample size increases, and that to compare means your sample size should be at least 30.

If our data is not normally distributed, we have three options: to transform our data (*e.g.* log transformation) to normalize the distribution, to use a nonparametric test to compare the means, or simply to use the *t*-test despite the non-normalcy of our data (the *t*-test is considered to be robust to violations of assumptions of normalcy).

The most common transformations used for non-normal data include logarithmic, square root, and reciprocal transformations. These transformations apply mathematical functions to the data, altering the scale and shape of the distribution to better approximate normality, allowing for more reliable analysis using parametric tests.

As can be observed in the graphs, two common Transformations to normalize data (Square root transformation (Y=SQRT(X), Log transformation (Y=log(X)) reduce the impact of extreme values and making the distribution more symmetric:

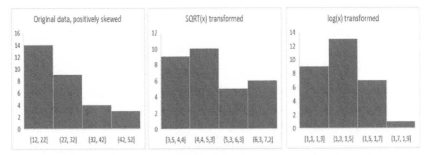

Figure 14.2: Transformation reduces the impact of extreme values and making the distribution more symmetric.

A further requirement for parametric tests is that of **homogeneity of variance**, meaning that the variances within the different treatments should be approximately equal. If one treatment is significantly more or less variable than the others, the analysis of variance (ANOVA) may not yield accurate results.

To determine if this requirement is met, and If you have access to a statistical package, you can use Bartlett's test or Levene's test to assess the equality of variances across multiple groups or samples. Bartlett's test performs well with larger sample sizes, and is more sensitive to deviations from normality, while Levene's test is suitable for both small and large sample sizes and is less sensitive and more robust in the presence of non-normality.

The F-test is commonly used in ANOVA to compare variances between groups assuming normality and equal variances.

Alternatively, a box and whisker graph can be examined, and you can critically evaluate your data by comparing the variability of samples using the Homogeneity of Variances Rule of Thumb:

Homogeneity of Variances Rule of Thumb: if the largest variance is no more than 4 times the small variance (i.e., if the largest standard deviation is less than two times the smallest standard deviation), you can assume the variance in each group is the same.

Outlier removal and Transformations to reduce variability

- Outlier removal eliminates extreme values that deviate significantly from the overall pattern of the data, reducing their impact and making the dataset more reliable. Q-test, IQR test, SD test
- Transformations to normalize data such as logarithmic transformation can help reduce the variability of skewed distributions or data with a wide range of values. Logarithmic transformations compress larger values more than smaller values, which can reduce the spread of the data and make it more symmetrical.

Parametric and non-parametric tests

For normally distributed data, standard parametric tests such as the T-test and ANOVA tests are typically used, while nonparametric tests are appropriate if the data does not follow the normal distribution.

Parametric tests assume a Normal or Gaussian distribution of Measurement data at the Interval or Ratio scales (see previous chapter), while nonparametric do not - although they are subject to sample size requirements (see below).

In addition to non-Gaussian Measurement data, Nonparametric tests are used for Categorical data at the Nominal or Ordinal scales.

As Parametric tests are more powerful than non-parametric tests and more likely to detect a significant effect when one indeed exists, many biologists tend to favor parametric tests rather than nonparametric tests, as any non-conformity to the prerequisites for parametric testing can often be circumvented through assumptions of normalcy, the identification and removal of outliers as well as data transformations.

In daily practice, it is thus usual for scientists to transform data from non-normal distributions, or to use parametric methods directly on datasets from non-normal distributions.

In cases where each treatment consists of fewer than 10 data values, as is common in crop protection studies, it is generally accepted that conducting tests for normal distribution becomes unreliable.

A biological rule of thumb is that the small data sets commonly found in lab and greenhouse trials may be assumed to be normally distributed and analyzed using standard parametric tests.

Therefore, neither data transformation nor the use of nonparametric tests would yield significant benefits. As a general rule of thumb in biology, small data sets commonly encountered in laboratory and greenhouse trials can be assumed to be Normally distributed, and standard parametric tests can be employed for analysis.

Overview of essential parametric and non-parametric methods

For hypothesis testing, specific parametric and nonparametric tests are available to evaluate different experimental datasets.

	Measurement (Gaussian) data	Categorical or Measurement (non-Gaussian) data
	Parametric	Nonparametric
Describe one group	Mean SD; SEM; 95%CI	Median Range
Compare one group to a hypothetical value	1-sample t-test	Wilcoxon test (or Chi-square for two possible outcomes)
Compare two unpaired groups	2-sample unpaired t-test	Mann-Whitney test
Compare two paired groups	2-sample paired t-test	Wilcoxon test
Compare three or more unmatched groups	One-Way ANOVA	Kruskal-Wallis test ((or Chi-square for two possible outcomes)
Predict value from measured values	*Linear or nonlinear regression*	*Nonparametric regression*

Figure 14.3: Overview of essential statistical analysis methods.

Among these, the most commonly used include tests to compare a single group of data to a hypothetical value, to compare two paired or unpaired groups, or to compare three or more groups, as well as the prediction of values from previously measured values.

NOTE: the information presented here comprises approximations and rules of thumb which are commonly used in designing and analyzing non-critical trials only. For critical experiments, nonparametric tests should be used if the data does not follow the

normal distribution (before or after transformation) or sample size requirements for
parametric tests - always seek the advice of a qualified statistician!

Microsoft Excel versus Statistics packages

This would be an appropriate time to spend a minute or two considering software packages for statistical data analysis. Microsoft Excel is perhaps the most commonly used data software in biological research and is often used (and misused) for Statistical Data Analysis.

Excel is first and foremost a spreadsheet with added data analysis modules, and it is important to understand that the software has limitations relative to professional statistic packages.

Excel is however excellent for data entry and data management and is accessible and sufficiently applicable for "quick-and-dirty" internal descriptive analyses and initial hypothesis testing carried out in research laboratories.

For more demanding applications (*e.g.* external reports and scientific papers) statisticians advise that Excel should only be used for data preparation, and this data should then be transferred to professional statistics packages for analysis. These results can then be reported directly or moved back to Excel for graphing and presentation purposes.

In Crop Protection Research, two of the most used data packages for trial planning and statistical data analysis are the commercial ARM (Agricultural Research Manager) package, and the open-source statistical package, R.

Both have relatively steep learning curves, but once they have been mastered, they become indispensable. For researchers with limited scientific knowledge, the GraphPad suite of statistical packages provides real-time guidance during data analysis.

We will obtain insight into the inferential methods commonly used to determine whether the means of the measured variables are equal (the null hypothesis) or whether they are significantly different (t-tests and ANOVA) in the following chapters.

———

15

TWO SAMPLE MEANS COMPARISON: THE T-TEST (PART I)

For biological experiments, the objective of most trials is to determine whether the means of the measured variables are equal (the null hypothesis) or whether they are significantly different.

The t-tests are a group of inferential parametric methods used to determine if two samples (or a sample and a theoretical mean) have the same mean (null hypothesis), or if there is a significant difference between the means.

The t-tests use the t-statistic (also termed t-value or t-ratio), t-distribution values and degrees of freedom to determine the difference probability between two data samples.

Different t-tests are used depending on whether a single sample is to be compared to a mean predicted by theory (one sample t-test), whether the samples are dependent (paired two-sample t-test) or independent (two-sample t-test) and whether the variances of the two samples are equal (two-sample t-test assuming equal variances) or not (two-sample t-test assuming unequal variances).

The one-sample t-test allows us to compare the mean of a single sample with an expected mean based on prior data (or a theoretical value), to determine if they are significantly different.

For example, if we - as part of an annual validation of our seed stocks - measured the mean weekly growth rate of ten seedlings from our in-house stock of spring barley seeds, we could compare this mean to last year's mean by performing a one-sample t-test to determine whether this year's mean growth rate was significantly different from last years recorded mean (the null hypothesis is that seedling vigor is unchanged, and that there will be no significant difference in weekly growth rate).

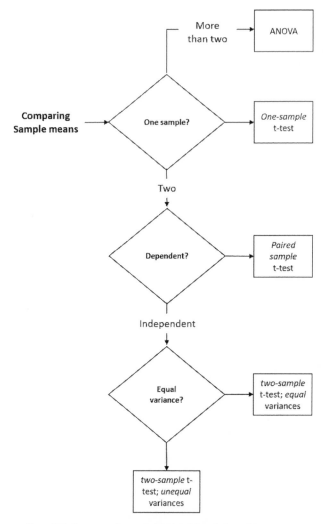

Figure 15.1: Summary of parametric inferential methods used to compare two sample means.

The paired *t*-test allows us to compare two sample means if each value within one sample can be paired with an associated value in the other, to determine if they are significantly different.

For example, if we measured the mean weekly growth rate of the same seedlings from our in-house stock of spring barley seeds over a period of consecutive weeks, we could compare this week's mean to last week's mean by performing a paired *t*-test to determine whether this week's mean growth rate is significantly different from last week's mean.

The (unpaired) two-sample *t*-test allows us to compare two sample means, to determine if they are significantly different.

For example, if we measured the mean weekly growth rate of herbicide-treated seedlings to untreated seedlings, we could use a two-sample *t*-test to determine whether the mean growth rate for the treated seedlings was significantly different from the untreated seedlings.

	One-sample *t*- test	Paired *t*- test	Two-sample *t*- test
	Single sample compared to predicted mean	*Two dependent samples*	*Two independent samples*
Sample variable:	Mean weekly growth rate *(current)*	Mean weekly growth rate *(this week)*	Mean weekly growth rate *(untreated)*
Compared variable:	Mean weekly growth rate *(last year)*	Mean weekly growth rate *(last week)*	Mean weekly growth rate *(treated)*

Figure 15.2: Example cases for one sample t-test for single data samples, paired two-sample t-test for dependent samples or two-sample t-test for independent samples.

The *t*-test assumes that the samples follow a normal (Gaussian) distribution.

A general rule of thumb is that the distribution of the mean approaches a normal distribution as sample size increases, and that to compare means your sample size should be at least 30.

For situations where a sample size of 30 is not feasible, the *t*-test was developed specifically to improve means testing results for small samples (typically less than 10 degrees of freedom).

Especially for samples with less than 5 degrees of freedom, the sharply increasing values of *t* (Figure 15.3) compensate for small sample size tendencies toward Type I errors (claiming a difference is significant when it is not).

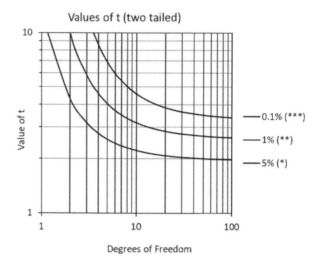

Figure 15.3: Values of t (two-tailed) for varying levels of significance.

Finally, the *t*-test **assumes that the data is sampled from populations that have equal variances,** even if their means are different.

As part of the (unpaired) two-sample *t*-test analysis, the *f*-test is used to determine if the two samples have equal variances - the topic of the next chapter.

———

16

TWO SAMPLE MEANS COMPARISONS: THE F-TEST

The (unpaired) two-sample t-test assumes that the data is sampled from populations that have equal variances, even if their means are different. As part of the (unpaired) two-sample t-test analysis, the f-test[1] is used to test if two samples have equal variances.

The f-test computes the ratio of the larger (greater) sample variance (square of the standard deviation, SD) relative to the smaller (lesser) variance. This f-ratio can be compared to one-tail critical f-table values ($\alpha = 0.05$) for n-1 degrees of freedom, df (Figure 16.1) to determine if the samples have the same values, $i.e.$ the computed f-ratio is smaller than the critical f-value.

		df (greater)										
		1	**2**	**3**	**4**	**5**	**6**	**7**	**8**	**9**	**10**	**20**	**∞**
df (lesser)	**1**	161	200	216	225	230	234	237	239	241	242	248	254
	2	18.5	19.0	19.2	19.3	19.3	19.3	19.4	19.4	19.4	19.4	19.4	19.5
	3	10.1	9.6	9.3	9.1	9.0	8.9	8.9	8.8	8.8	8.8	8.7	8.5
	4	7.7	6.9	6.6	6.4	6.3	6.2	6.1	6.0	6.0	6.0	5.8	5.6
	5	6.6	5.8	5.4	5.2	5.1	5.0	4.9	4.8	4.8	4.7	4.6	4.4
	6	5.6	5.1	4.8	4.5	4.4	4.3	4.2	4.2	4.1	4.1	3.9	3.7
	7	5.6	4.7	4.4	4.1	4.0	3.9	3.8	3.7	3.7	3.6	3.4	3.3
	8	5.3	4.5	4.1	3.8	3.7	3.6	3.5	3.4	3.4	3.4	3.2	2.9
	9	5.1	4.3	3.9	3.6	3.5	3.4	3.3	3.2	3.2	3.1	2.9	2.8
	10	5.0	4.1	3.7	3.5	3.3	3.2	3.1	3.1	3.0	3.0	2.8	2.5
	20	4.4	3.5	3.1	2.9	2.7	2.6	2.5	2.5	2.4	2.4	2.1	1.8
	∞	3.8	3.0	2.6	2.4	2.2	2.1	2.0	1.9	1.9	1.8	1.6	1.0

Figure 16.1: One-tailed f-table for $\alpha = 0.05$.

As $\alpha = 0.05$ corresponds to a 5% (or less) chance of discarding the null hypothesis (the samples have equal variances), if the computed value is less than the table value the null hypothesis may not be discarded *i.e.* the samples have equal variances.

If this is the case, the two sample means may be compared using the two-sample *t*-test for *equal* variances; alternatively, the two-sample *t*-test for *unequal* variances should be chosen.

Example: Comparing treated and untreated seedlings.

In the following example, the mean height of ten untreated seedlings is compared to the mean height of ten herbicidally treated seedlings.

The means of the two sample data sets are respectively 62 cm and 48 cm (Figure 16.2), and we wish to determine if the two samples have the same mean (null hypothesis), or if there is a significant difference between the means.

As we have two samples which are unpaired, an (unpaired) two-sample *t*-test will allow us to compare the two sample means, to determine if they are significantly different.

The next step is to use the *f*-test to determine whether the variances of the two samples are equal or not.

Untreated	Treated
63	53
72	48
54	43
62	45
57	55
73	47
53	41
51	57
61	53
69	39
Mean: 62	48

Figure 16.2: Experimental sample data; mean height of ten untreated and herbicide-treated seedlings.

The ratio of the greater sample variance relative to the lesser variance (f-ratio) is 60.7/38.0 = 1.6, which is less than the table value of 3.2 for n-1 degrees of freedom *i.e.* 9df (Figure 16.3).

As the f-ratio is lower than the critical f value, we may conclude that the variances of the two samples are equal.

Untreated	Treated
63	53
72	48
54	43
62	45
57	55
73	47
53	41
51	57
61	53
69	39
Mean: 62	48

	Untreated	Treated
Mean	61.58	48.12
Variance	60.68	37.96
Observations	10	10
df	9	9
F	1.6	
P(F<=f) one-tail	0.25	
F Critical one-tail	3.2	

		df (greater)										
		1	2	3	4	5	6	7	8	9	10	20	∞
df (Lesser)	1	161	200	216	225	230	234	237	239	241	242	248	254
	2	18.5	19.0	19.2	19.3	19.3	19.3	19.4	19.4	19.4	19.4	19.4	19.5
	3	10.1	9.6	9.3	9.1	9.0	8.9	8.9	8.8	8.8	8.8	8.7	8.5
	4	7.7	6.9	6.6	6.4	6.3	6.2	6.1	6.0	6.0	6.0	5.8	5.6
	5	6.6	5.8	5.4	5.2	5.1	5.0	4.9	4.8	4.8	4.7	4.6	4.4
	6	5.6	5.1	4.8	4.5	4.4	4.3	4.2	4.2	4.1	4.1	3.9	3.7
	7	5.6	4.7	4.4	4.1	4.0	3.9	3.8	3.7	3.7	3.6	3.4	3.3
	8	5.3	4.5	4.1	3.8	3.7	3.6	3.5	3.4	3.4	3.4	3.2	2.9
	9	5.1	4.3	3.9	3.6	3.5	3.4	3.3	3.2	3.2	3.1	2.9	2.8
	10	5.0	4.1	3.7	3.5	3.3	3.2	3.1	3.1	3.0	3.0	2.8	2.5
	20	4.4	3.5	3.1	2.9	2.7	2.6	2.5	2.5	2.4	2.4	2.1	1.8
	∞	3.8	3.0	2.6	2.4	2.2	2.1	2.0	1.9	1.9	1.8	1.6	1.0

Figure 16.3: Result of f-test to determine equivalence of variance for two experimental data samples (calculated in Excel).

Statistical software packages provide convenient f-test functions for determining equality of variance and provide a p-value (the chance that the variances of the two samples are equal).

A small p-value (<0.05) indicates that the chance that the variances of the two samples are equal is small, and that the variances are thus different.

For our sample data, a p-value of 0.25 (>0.05) thus confirms our table-based finding that the variances of the two samples are equal, and we may proceed to compare the two means using the two-sample t-test for equal variances. Alternatively, we would choose a modification of this test - the two-sample t-test for *unequal* variances.

Implementation of the t-test to determine if two samples (or a sample and a theoretical mean) have the same mean, or if there is a significant difference between the means, will be discussed in the next chapter.

---

1. The f-test was initially developed by Fisher as the variance ratio (defined as the ratio of explained variance (or between-group variability) to unexplained variance (or within-group variability) in the 1920s. The f-distribution was subsequently tabulated, and the f-test named, by Snedecor in 1934 as an improved presentation of Fisher's Analysis of Variance, in order to facilitate its interpretation within the biological sciences.

17

TWO SAMPLE MEANS COMPARISONS: THE T-TEST (PART II)

The test statistic for all t-tests (one sample, paired two-sample or independent two-sample t-tests) is the t-value or t-ratio, which is the difference between the sample means (numerator) divided by the standard error of the difference (denominator)[1].

Expressed in other terms - the numerator is the effect size (signal) and the denominator is the variability (noise) while the t-value may be considered to represent the signal:noise ratio.

The t-values are calculated differently for each test:

For a one-sample t-test, the expected or theoretical mean is subtracted from the mean of the sample, and this is divided by the standard error of the sample. The degrees of freedom (df) used in this test are n−1. For a sample of 10 seedlings, the degrees of freedom are thus [10-1=9].

For paired two-sample t-tests, the difference between the sample means is divided by the standard error of the mean differences. As the difference between the sample means is the same as a single sample (the mean differences), the degrees of freedom (df) used in this test are n-1. For two paired samples of 10 seedlings, the degrees of freedom are thus [10-1=9].

For two-sample t-tests, the difference between the sample means is divided by the pooled (averaged) standard error for the two samples (which in turn explains the need for an assumption of equal variances for the two samples). The degrees of freedom (df) used in this test are [n (sample 1) + n (sample 2) −

2]. For two samples of 10 seedlings, the degrees of freedom are thus [10+10-2=8].

As statistical software packages (and most spreadsheets) provide convenient *t*-test functions, we will not delve deeper into the calculation of *t*, but rather focus on interpreting the results.

Example: Comparing treated and untreated seedlings.

In our sample data (see previous chapter) of the height of ten untreated seedlings compared to the height of ten herbicide-treated seedlings, the *f*-test was used to determine whether the variances of the two samples were equal or not.

As the *f*-ratio was smaller than the critical *f*-value, we could conclude that the variances of the two samples were equal and that we may compare the means using the *two-sample t-test for equal variances* and calculate or compute the *t*-value (Figure 17.1). Had the variances not been equal, we would choose the two-sample *t*-test for unequal variances.

Untreated	Treated
63	53
72	48
54	43
62	45
57	55
73	47
53	41
51	57
61	53
69	39

	Untreated	Treated
Mean	61.6	48.1
Variance	60.68	37.96
Observations	10	10
Pooled Variance	49.32	
Hypothesized Mean Difference	0	
df	18	
t Stat	4.29	
P(T<=t) one-tail	0.0002	
t Critical one-tail	1.734	
P(T<=t) two-tail	0.0004	
t Critical two-tail	2.10	

Figure 17.1: Result of two-sample t-test for equal variances (with p-values) to compare means for two experimental data samples (calculated in Excel; top)

To interpret the results, the calculated *t*-value can be compared to *two-tail critical t table values* (Figure 17.2) for n-2 degrees of freedom (the total sample size of 10+10-2=18df) to determine whether the sample means are equal (or significantly different).

df	p= .05 2-tailed	df	p= .05 2-tailed
1	12.71	13	2.16
2	4.30	14	2.14
3	3.18	15	2.13
4	2.78	16	2.12
5	2.57	17	2.11
6	2.45	18	2.10
7	2.36	19	2.09
8	2.31	20	2.09
9	2.26	30	2.04
10	2.23	50	2.01
11	2.20	100	1.98
12	2.18	∞	1.96

Figure 17.2: Critical t-values for p= 0.05; two-tailed.

As p=0.05 corresponds to a 5% (or less) chance of discarding the null hypothesis (the means are equal), *t*-values less than the critical table value mean the null hypothesis may not be discarded *i.e.* the samples have equal means.

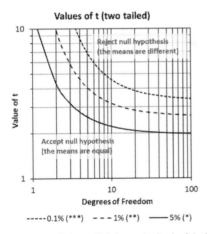

Figure 17.3: Values of t (two-tailed) for varying levels of significance.

In our example, the t-value (4.29) is greater than the critical t-value ($t=2.10$ for 18df), and we may thus conclude that the means of the two samples are significantly different.

Similarly, for our sample data a computed p-value of <0.05 (Figure 17.1) confirms that the means of the two samples are significantly different.

While t-tests allow us to determine if two samples have the same mean, biological experiments usually comprise more than two samples.

Accordingly, Analysis of Variance (ANOVA) tests are used to evaluate multiple (three or more) data samples, and this is the subject of the next chapter.

---

1. William Sealy Gosset (1876-1937), a chemist and statistician at the Guinness Brewery introduced the z-statistic to test the means of small, normally-distributed samples for quality control in brewing, and published it anonymously under the name "Student".

   Gosset's test was adapted by R.A. Fisher to incorporate the concept of "degrees of freedom" (introduced by him in its statistical context) in a 1924 paper, and Gosset appears to have introduced the t-nomenclature (t-distribution; t-test) in correspondence with Fisher. The t-statistic is also termed Students t-distribution and Students t-test.

18

MULTIPLE SAMPLE MEANS COMPARISONS: ANOVA TEST

While the t-test is used to compare the means of two treatments, samples or groups, Analysis of Variance (ANOVA[1]) are hypothesis tests used to differentiate between the means of more than two treatments, or groups.

Using ANOVA to compare two groups will return the same results (p-value) as using the t-test. Although it may seem simpler to compare the means of multiple samples as a series of multiple two-sample comparisons (t-tests), this is not a recommended option as increasing the number of comparisons compounds the error, and we risk making a type-I error *i.e.* falsely concluding a significant difference when there is no real difference.

The objective of the ANOVA test is thus to allow us to perform a single comparison test to compare multiple groups of data, thereby reducing the chance of making a type-I error.

As the mathematics required of the ANOVA tests are beyond the scope of this book, and as the tests can now be conveniently performed through spreadsheets, online calculators and dedicated statistical programs, we will in the following focus on understanding the underlying assumptions as well as the output of the ANOVA tests.

The most common application of ANOVA in crop protection R&D is the one-way ANOVA, used to differentiate between the means of more than two treatments, for which there is one measurement variable (*e.g.* plant height) and one nominal variable, or factor (*e.g.* pesticide).

TEST	TREATMENTS	FACTORS	EXAMPLE
t-test	Two treatments	One factor: e.g. pesticide treatment	Control vs. treated
One-way ANOVA			Untreated control, treatment A; treatment B
Two-way ANOVA	More than two treatments	Two factors: e.g. pesticide treatment and location	Three or more treatments, and two locations
Three-way ANOVA		Three factors: e.g. pesticide treatment, location and pest development stage	Three or more treatments, two locations with target pests from two development stages

Figure 18.1: Summary of Means comparisons.

Two- and three-way ANOVA tests are used to differentiate between the means of more than two treatments, for which there is one measurement variable and two (or three) nominal variables, or factors (Figure 18.1).

Assumption of Normality and Homogeneity of Variance

As is the case for the t-test, ANOVA assumes that the data is sampled from populations that have equal variance. Tests such as Bartlett's test for homogeneity of variance are typically used to test this assumption - if Bartlett's test reveals deviances from homogeneity, data transformation can be considered.

Both Bartlett's as well as the ANOVA test assume that the samples follow a normal (Gaussian) distribution (see previous chapters). A number of tests of normality are available, such as the Shapiro–Wilk and Kolmogorov–Smirnov tests, but these require statistical insight or access to statistical software packages.

If each treatment comprises less than ten data values, a general assumption (previously described as the Normality Rule of Thumb) is that any test of normal distribution will be so compromised that neither data transformation nor the use of nonparametric tests (*e.g.* the Kruskal-Wallis test, see chapter 12: "Nonparametric or Parametric Statistical Tests") will provide a significant benefit.

In daily practice, however, it is common for scientists to simply use parametric methods such as the ANOVA test directly on datasets from non-normal distributions.

Understanding the output of ANOVA tests

ANOVA differentiates between treatment (group) means by using the f-ratio to compare variance within and between treatments or groups - if the variation (typically termed "error") *within* groups is greater than the variation *between* groups, the difference between the means is not considered significant.

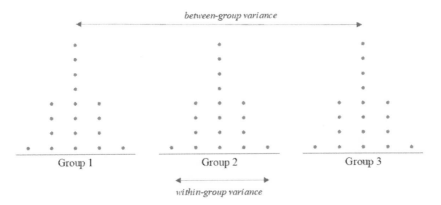

Figure 18.2: Between-group and within-group variance.

In the following example (Figure 18.3), we use the dataset for plant heights for ten untreated seedlings and ten herbicidally-treated seedlings (Treatment A) used in the previous chapter and expand it by adding an extra treatment (Treatment B), for a total of three groups (untreated control plus two treatments).

To calculate the within-group and between-group variance, the dispersion of the data (*Sum of Squares; SS*) was divided by the Degrees of Freedom (*df*) to give the variance (*Mean Square; MS*).

Degrees of freedom are calculated *between* groups (*m-1*) as 3 groups minus 1 = 2 and *within* groups (*n-m*) as 30 observations (*n*) minus 3 groups (*m*) = 27.

The f-ratio (F) is the ratio of the between-groups variance (*MS_between*) divided by the within-groups variance (*MS_within*), and the calculated ratio is compared to distribution values (one-tail critical f-table values) in order to determine significance (Figure 18.4).

Untreated	Treatment A	Treatment B
63	53	45
72	48	41
54	43	37
62	45	33
57	55	34
73	47	45
53	41	50
51	57	39
61	53	42
69	39	52

SUMMARY

Groups	Count	Sum	Average	Variance
Untreated	10	615.78	61.578	60.68
Treatment A	10	481.2	48.12	37.96
Treatment B	10	418	41.8	40.18

ANOVA

Source of Variation	SS	df	MS	F	P-value	F crit
Between Groups	2041	2	1020	22	0.0000021	3.35
Within Groups	1249	27	46			
Total	3290	29				

Figure 18.3: ANOVA output (Excel) comparing plant heights (cm) of untreated and treated plants.

As the f-ratio of the between-groups variance relative to the within-groups variance ($F = 22$) is greater than the table value of 3.35 (F crt) for 2 df between groups and 27 df within groups, we may conclude that there is a significant difference between the means of the treatments being compared.

For manual calculations of the f-ratio, significance may be determined using the f-table (figure 18.4).

However, statistical packages, spreadsheets and online ANOVA calculators supplement f-ratios and critical values with a P value (the chance that the means are equal).

If the p-value is less than 0.05, we may reject the null hypothesis that the means are equal and conclude that there is a significant difference between the means.

Likewise, if the p-value is greater than 0.05, we may accept the null hypothesis and conclude that there is no significant difference between the means.

df (between groups or treatments)											
1	**2**	**3**	**4**	**5**	**6**	**7**	**8**	**9**	**10**	**20**	**∞**
161	200	216	225	230	234	237	239	241	242	248	254
18.5	19.0	19.2	19.3	19.3	19.3	19.4	19.4	19.4	19.4	19.4	19.5
10.1	9.6	9.3	9.1	9.0	8.9	8.9	8.8	8.8	8.8	8.7	8.5
7.7	6.9	6.6	6.4	6.3	6.2	6.1	6.0	6.0	6.0	5.8	5.6
6.6	5.8	5.4	5.2	5.1	5.0	4.9	4.8	4.8	4.7	4.6	4.4
5.6	5.1	4.8	4.5	4.4	4.3	4.2	4.2	4.1	4.1	3.9	3.7
5.6	4.7	4.4	4.1	4.0	3.9	3.8	3.7	3.7	3.6	3.4	3.3
5.3	4.5	4.1	3.8	3.7	3.6	3.5	3.4	3.4	3.4	3.2	2.9
5.1	4.3	3.9	3.6	3.5	3.4	3.3	3.2	3.2	3.1	2.9	2.8
5.0	4.1	3.7	3.5	3.3	3.2	3.1	3.1	3.0	3.0	2.8	2.5
4.4	3.5	3.1	2.9	2.7	2.6	2.5	2.5	2.4	2.4	2.1	1.8
3.8	3.0	2.6	2.4	2.2	2.1	2.0	1.9	1.9	1.8	1.6	1.0

(Row labels df within groups: 1, 2, 3, 4, 5, 6, 7, 8, 9, 10, 20, ∞)

Figure 18.4: One-tailed f-table for α = 0.05

In our example above, we can determine that the p-value is considerably less than 0.001 (*i.e.* the difference between the means is extremely significant). However, the results of the ANOVA test only indicate if there is a significant difference between means, and do not reveal *which* group is different nor *how* it is different.

To determine this, we need to supplement the ANOVA test with post-hoc ("done after the event") or post-ANOVA tests for significant differences.

Post-ANOVA (post-hoc) tests

Post-ANOVA tests are typically performed after the f-ratio has indicated that not all means are equal.

Depending on our requirements, different post-ANOVA tests allow different comparisons, for example: to compare every mean to every other mean (the most common application), to compare each mean to a control mean, or to compare selected means.

Among the post-ANOVA tests to compare every mean to every other mean, we are provided with a number of methods, the most common of which (at least in the biological sciences) are the Tukey's test and the Newman-Keuls test (or Student-Newman-Keuls test; SNK).

The Newman-Keuls post-ANOVA test is considered less stringent (has less power - see previous chapter on Power) than Tukey's test, and may indicate that a difference in means is statistically significant, whereas the more stringent Tukey's test might indicate that the difference is not statistically significant.

As the risk of a Type-I error (where there really is no difference) is greater for the Newman-Keuls test than for the Tukey test, statisticians tend to recommend Tukey's test.

However, for Tukey's test the chance of a Type-II error (missing a real difference) is greater. This is the "one that got away" type error, also termed "false negative", where you miss out on something that really is extraordinary.

POST-ANOVA TEST	STRINGENCY	RISK
Tukey's test	More stringent: "there is no difference"	Type-II error (missing a real difference; false negative)
Newman-Keuls, or SNK	Less stringent: "there is a difference"	Type-I error (where there really is no difference; false positive)

Figure 18.5: Summary of post-ANOVA tests most commonly used to identify differences between all group means.

Taking the strategic research objectives into consideration will facilitate a reasoned choice of test method. Thus, if the cost of a false positive is high (for example if it leads to the initiation of a costly development process) a more stringent method to determine the significance of differences between treatment means such as Tukey's test may be appropriate.

Conversely, if the cost of a false negative is high (leading to you missing out on a valuable discovery) a less stringent method such as Newman-Keuls test may be appropriate.

Newman-Keuls test may thus be appropriate for early stage discovery processes, while Tukey's may be more appropriate as a decision-making tool as discovery candidates approach development phases.

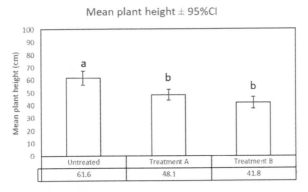

Figure 18.6: Mean plant heights for untreated control and two herbicide treatments. Different letters above bars indicate significant differences (p<0.05; Tukey's post-ANOVA test).

The means and results of post-ANOVA tests are typically presented as bar graphs (with error bars correctly defined), where different letters above bars (means) indicate significant differences (p<0.05). Conversely, bars labeled with the same letter are not significantly different from each other.

In contrast, applying the SNK test to the example dataset (Figure 18.7) confirms that the means of treatment A and Treatment B are significantly different from that of the untreated control (p<0.001) while the lower stringency of this tests indicates that the difference between the means of Treatment A and Treatment B is significantly different (p<0.05):

A number of additional post-ANOVA tests are available for specific comparisons (to compare each mean to a control mean, or to compare selected means, *e.g.* Bonferroni's test), or for situations for which the assumption of equal variances may (*e.g.* Duncan's test - a more stringent modification of the Newman-Keuls test *i.e.* with more power) or may not (*e.g.* Dunnett's test) be required.

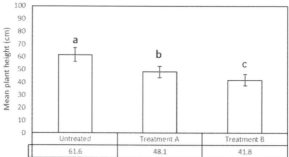

Figure 18.7: Mean plant heights for untreated control and two herbicide treatments. Different letters above bars indicate significant differences (p<0.05; SNK post-ANOVA test).

These necessitate an in-depth understanding of statistical analysis and are thus outside the scope of this book - the reader is encouraged to refer to a statistician.

---

1. One of British statistician and geneticist R.A. Fisher's (1892-1962) most important contributions to statistical methods is the analysis of variance (ANOVA), providing solutions to issues of variance arising from factors such as the heterogeneity of soils and the variability of biological material. Several of his most important contributions were published in "Statistical methods for research workers" (1925).

V

NONLINEAR AND LINEAR REGRESSION

19

NON-LINEAR REGRESSION (SIGMOIDAL DOSE-RESPONSES)

Bioassays (analytical methods to determine the potency of a substance by its effect on living organisms) are used in all fields of the biological sciences - from the agricultural sciences over toxicology and biochemistry to medicine - for the assessment of biological activity and selectivity of pesticides, biochemicals and pharmaceuticals.

Bioassays include dose-response studies using several (typically replicated) doses of one or more biologically active compounds, or active ingredient (a.i.) to measure the response of specific target organisms.

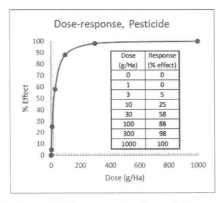

Figure 19.1: Hyperbolic dose-response (effect) curve for linear, arithmetic doses. Insert: Dose-response data table.

In dose-response experiments, an active ingredient's (*e.g.* herbicide) effect on a target organism (plant) is typically investigated by constructing a dose-response curve which describes the relationship between increasing the dose and the associated change in response across a dose range.

On an arithmetic (linear) scale, the dose is plotted on the X-axis and response is plotted on the Y-axis, and the response curve is hyperbolic.

On this linear scale, it is apparent that evaluating the transition from low to high response is difficult, as most of the information is compressed in a small section of the graph.

To address this, the doses on the X-axis may be logarithmically transformed.

On a logarithmic dose scale (see Figure 19.2), dose-responses typically follow the classic sigmoidal curve familiar to biologists from *e.g.* bacterial growth studies.

Sigmoidal dose-response fitting

From the approximately linear slope of the sigmoidal dose-response fit (from approximately 10-20% effect to 80-90% effect, over about two log units) we can derive Effective Dose levels (EDx), *i.e.* the doses causing a specific response x in the target organism.

Among these are the Effective Dose, ED50 (for example, herbicide dose required to reduce for example plant growth by 50%, *i.e.* half-way between the upper and lower asymptote; see Figure 19.2), ED10 (dose required to reduce plant growth by 50%, often defined as the No Observable Effect Level; NOEL) and ED90.

Other terminology used includes EC (Effective Concentration), LC/LD (lethal concentration/dose, for toxicology) and IC (inhibitory concentration, for biochemistry).

Pesticide dose-response experiments typically use 5-7 doses, equally spaced on a logarithmic scale. For example, doses might be 1, 3, 10, 30, 100, 300, 1000 g ai/Ha. When converted to logarithms, these values are equally spaced: 0.0, 0.5, 1.0, 1.5, 2.0, 2.5, 3.0.

This provides a sufficiently broad and equally spaced range of doses to ensure zero percent effect at the lower asymptote (plateau) and 100% effect at the upper asymptote - requirements for fitting the sigmoidal dose-response curve (see below).

For some trials (especially insecticide trials) mortality may arise for the untreated "control" due to natural causes, and Schneider-Orelli's formula may be used to correct for control response (typically mortality) if control response is more than 10% (see also chapter 12)

In its basic form, the standard sigmoidal dose-response curve showing response (Y) as a function of the logarithm of concentration (X) may be fitted by eye or by the following equation:

$$Y=Bottom+ \frac{(Top-Bottom)}{(1+10^{(logEC50-x)})}$$

...where "Top" is the response at the upper asymptote (the response at high doses), "Bottom" is the response at the lower asymptote (response to the untreated control) and logEC50 is the logarithm of the EC50 (the dose giving a response half-way between the upper and lower asymptotes).

The number 1 indicates the standard slope (termed Hill slope) where the response increases linearly from approximately 10-20% to 80-90% of maximal as the dose increases over about two log units.

Dose (g/Ha)	log Dose	Response (% effect)
0.1	-1	0
1	0	0
3	0.5	5
10	1	25
30	1.5	58
100	2	88
300	2.5	98
1000	3	100

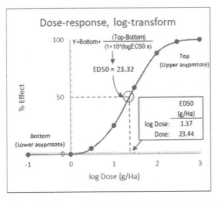

Figure 19.2: Sigmoidal dose-response (effect) curve for log-transformed doses, visual estimation and calculation of ED50. Top: transformed dose-response data table.

In our example above, using values from a herbicide dose-response curve, the

ED50 value may be fitted by eye as logED50 = 1.37 from which the dose may be determined as ED50 = 10^1.37 = 23.44g ai / Ha.

Alternatively, the ED50 value may be calculated (using *e.g.* a statistics package) as ED50 = 23.22g ai / Ha.

Here, both values are almost equal, as the data conveniently fits the sigmoidal curve - for data with more scatter around the regression line, visual determination of ED50 becomes less precise.

A further advantage of using statistical packages is that goodness-of-fit of the data to the regression curve can be quantified.

The standard sigmoidal dose-response curve assumes a standard Hill slope, but in practice, a revised equation for variable slopes is often used.

Theoretically, the slope should be equal when evaluating different formulations of the same active ingredient, and different when evaluating different formulations of the same active ingredient.

Often, experimenters will not have enough data to allow accurate curve fitting, and confidence intervals of the fit may be used to approach best-fit slope parameters. Alternatively, an extrapolated data value (typically 2 or three orders of magnitude higher than the expected 100% efficacy rate may be extrapolated.

These advanced cases (including biphasic dose-response curves) lie outside the scope of this book, but most statistical packages are able to fit these conditions.

If statistical software packages are not available, and experimenters do not have a background in mathematics, linear dose-response fitting may be conveniently performed using PROBIT models. This will be the topic of the next chapter.

———

20

LINEAR REGRESSION (PROBIT)

Probit ("probability unit") models were developed by American biologist and statistician Chester Bliss in 1934, as a method to evaluate dose response in pesticide data.

Probit allows researchers to convert mortality (effect) percentages to probit values, which approximate a straight line function between the logarithm of the dose and effect, and which can be analyzed by simple linear regression methods.

Probit is thus the transformation of the sigmoid dose-response curve to a straight line.

The Probit model was further adapted and tabulated at Rothamsted by British statisticians D. J. Finney and W. L. Stevens in 1948 to avoid having to work with negative probits in an era before the ready availability of electronic computing.

It is these Probit tables that even today ensure that dose-response fitting to evaluate dose-response relationships may be conveniently performed when statistical software packages are not available, and experimenters do not have a background in mathematics.

Probit analysis may be conducted using tables to determine the probits and fitting the relationship by eye or through linear regression, or by using a statistical package. The process for evaluating dose-response relationships through the Probit analysis by hand, or by using a spreadsheet, are outlined in the following:

Step 1: log transform the doses.

Step 2: Convert % response to probits (short for probability unit).

Probits are generally calculated in the range where the sigmoidal response increases linearly *i.e.* from approximately 10-20% to 80-90% of maxima and should ideally contain three points within this linear phase.

If control (untreated) response is more than 10%, Schneider-Orelli's correction (see previous chapter) may be used. Probits for a given percentage effect may be determined using Finney's table:

%	1	2	3	4	5	6	7	8	9
0	–	2.67	2.95	3.12	3.25	3.36	3.45	3.52	3.59	3.66
10	3.72	3.77	3.83	3.87	3.92	3.96	4.01	4.05	4.08	4.12
20	4.16	4.19	4.23	4.26	4.29	4.33	4.36	4.39	4.42	4.45
30	4.48	4.50	4.53	4.56	4.59	4.61	4.64	4.67	4.69	4.72
40	4.75	4.77	4.80	4.82	4.85	4.87	4.90	4.92	4.95	4.97
50	5.00	5.03	5.05	5.08	5.10	5.13	5.15	5.18	5.20	5.23
60	5.25	5.28	5.31	5.33	5.36	5.39	5.41	5.44	5.47	5.50
70	5.52	5.55	5.58	5.61	5.64	5.67	5.71	5.74	5.77	5.81
80	5.84	5.88	5.92	5.95	5.99	6.04	6.08	6.13	6.17	6.23
90	6.28	6.34	6.41	6.48	6.55	6.64	6.75	6.88	7.05	7.33

Figure 20.1 Finney's table for the transformation of response percentages to probits.

In our example, for a 25% response the corresponding probit is 4.33, for 58% effect probit=5.20 and for 88% effect probit=6.18:

Dose (g/Ha)	log Dose	Response (% effect)	Probit
0.1	-1	0	
1	0	0	
3	0.48	5	
10	1	25	4.33
30	1.48	58	5.20
100	2	88	6.18
300	2.48	98	
1000	3	100	

Figure 20.2: Dose-response data table, log-transformed doses and transformation of response percentages to probits.

Step 3: Graph the probits versus the log of the concentrations and perform a linear regression, by hand or using a spreadsheet (Figure 20.3).

Step 4: Determine the ED50.

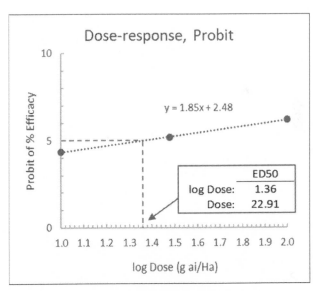

Figure 20.3: Linear fit of dose-response data, probits versus the log of the concentrations: visual estimation of ED50.

In our example, using values from a herbicide dose-response curve, the ED50 value may be fitted by eye as logED50= 1.36 from which the dose may be determined as ED50= 10^1.36= 22.91g ai/Ha:

Alternatively, if the linear function has been calculated (in our example as y= 1.85x + 2.48) the ED50 may be calculated as:

$$\log \text{Dose} = \frac{\text{Probit value - intercept}}{\text{Slope}}$$

...where 2.48 is the intercept (at x=0) and 1.85 is the slope. The Probit value is 5 for ED50 (in Finney's table, Figure 20.1, for a 50% response (ED50) the corresponding probit is 5):

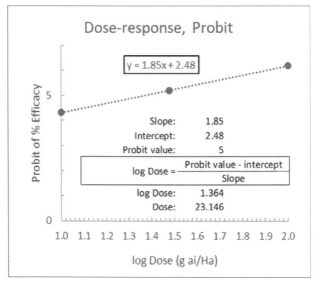

Figure 20.4: Linear fit of dose-response data, probits versus the log of the concentrations: calculation of ED50.

In our example, logED50= 1.364 from which the dose may be determined as ED50= 10^1.364= 23.146g ai/Ha.

An alternative method of calculating Effective Dose levels (ED*x*) is Logit, which can be performed through a similar process to that described for Probit.

The key difference between logit and probit models lies in the assumption of the distribution of the errors, where for probit the errors are assumed to follow a Normal distribution. In practice, both generally lead to the same conclusions and both are thus considered appropriate.

In our example, for both non-linear (sigmoidal) regression (see previous chapter) and linear (Probit) regression, both ED50 values are almost equal, and visual estimates were relatively accurate. For data with more scatter around the regression line, visual determination of ED50 becomes less precise.

As for non-linear regression, a further advantage of using statistical packages is that the goodness-of-fit of the data to the regression curve can be quantified.

———

21

AREA UNDER THE DISEASE PROGRESS CURVE (AUDPC)

Most plant pathogens are polycyclic, with recurring production of inoculum and reinfection leading to increases in the disease during the growing season.

By evaluating disease levels over time, it is possible to combine multiple observations from disease progress experiments into a single cumulative value (a measure of duration and intensity) by integrating the Area Under the Disease Progress Curve (AUDPC).

AUDPC is used in crop protection efficacy studies to compare levels of efficacy between treatments over time.

To obtain the AUDPC, disease evaluations commence when the symptoms appear, typically when the untreated control plots reach 20% disease severity and are repeated at 3-10 day intervals (days after treatment, DAT) until disease severity passes 80%, to ensure data is available for low, medium and high disease severity.

Ideally the AUDPC would be calculated through integration, although the midpoint method provides a simple estimate of the area under the infection curve.

The midpoint method approximates the area between the infection curve and the x-axis by summing the areas of rectangles with midpoints that are points on the curve between evaluations times.:

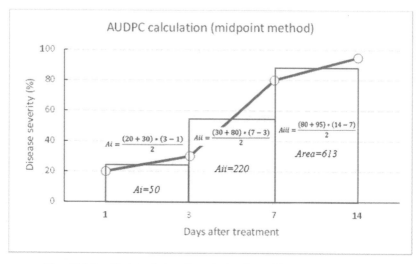

Figure 21.1: the midpoint method provides a simple estimate of the area under the infection curve.

The midpoint method is expressed as:

$$A(UDPC) = \frac{(SEV1 + SEV2) * (T1 - T2)}{2}$$

where SEV = disease severity and T = evaluation times (DAT) for two evaluations typically made at 3-10 day intervals.

Example: calculating AUDPC using the midpoint rule

For a treatment A, the following disease severity evaluations were made at four timepoints following application of treatment A:

Treatment	Days after treatment (DAT)			
	1	3	7	14
A	20	30	80	95

Step 1) add the first and second score (20 and 30)

Step 2) multiply by the time between them (50 x 2 days=100) and divide by two (=50).

Step 3) Repeat for second and third score: 30 + 80 = 110. 110 x 4 = 440.

Step 4) Divide by 2 = 220.

Step 5) Repeat for all consecutive pairs of scores and add the values together to determine the AUDPC:

$$Ai = \frac{(20 + 30) * (3 - 1)}{2} = 50$$

$$Aii = \frac{(30 + 80) * (7 - 3)}{2} = 220$$

$$Aiii = \frac{(80 + 95) * (14 - 7)}{2} = 613$$

$$AUDPC = Ai + Aii + Aiii = 883$$

Example: comparing treatments over time using AUDPC

In this example, the efficacy of three fungicides (ABC) is compared at multiple timepoints over the duration of the infection by evaluating disease severity at 1, 3, 7 and 14 days after treatment:

Treatment	Days after treatment (DAT)			
	1	3	7	14
A	25	25	40	97
B	20	20	70	97
C	30	45	71	97

The data can be graphically presented as:

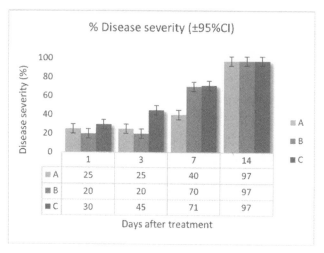

Figure 21.2: Results of efficacy trial, multiple observations from disease
progress experiments.

For trials with multiple treatments and evaluations, it can be beneficial to
create an overview and rank the treatments by combining multiple
observations from disease progress experiments into a single, cumulative
AUDPC value:

	Days after treatment (DAT)				AUDPC			
Treatment	1	3	7	14	1-3DAT	3-7DAT	7-14DAT	Total
A	25	25	40	97	50	130	480	660
B	20	20	70	97	40	180	585	805
C	30	45	71	97	75	232	588	895

In this example, treatment A is the most effective (lowest AUDPC) while
treatment C is the least effective (greatest AUDPC).

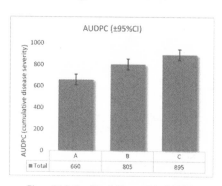

Figure 21.3: Results of efficacy trial, AUDPC.

While the advantage of AUDPC is to combine multiple observations of disease progress into a single value, this method tends to underestimate the effect of the first and last observations (upper and lower asymptotes).

This is a characteristic of the sigmoid curve and was identified in the previous chapter for EC50 calculation and will be reencountered in the following chapter on synergy.

This shortcoming may be alleviated by restricting the AUDPC calculation to the range between 20% and 80% disease severity i.e., to the linear phase of the curve.

———

VI

SYNERGY

22

DEMONSTRATING SYNERGY FROM EFFICACY DATA

Active ingredient mixes can extend the patent life of mixture partners and thus defend the market position. A synergistic effect is defined as whenever the action of a combination of active ingredients is greater than the sum of the actions of the individual components.

Not only is synergism an accepted argument against any allegation of obviousness in patent applications, but active ingredient synergism also allows better pest, pathogen or weed control with equal or reduced active ingredient rates. However, there is a risk that synergism could cause injury to crops or other non-target plants.

Synergy vs. formulation differences

Efficacy and synergy are determined not only by the active ingredients but also by the absence or presence of formulation inerts - solvents, adjuvants etc. Ideally, the individual active ingredients and the mix of actives should be formulated in the same way, to eliminate the effects of differing formulation inerts on biological activity.

In practice, however, it is common to observe mixes of formulated commercial products in patent applications, despite the issues of potential increased effect due to the combination of adjuvants in the commercial products - if there is no alternative, be prepared to demonstrate that differing formulation inerts have no effect on biological activity.

. . .

Models used to demonstrate synergy

In crop protection, two reference models are commonly used to demonstrate synergy: the Multiplicative Survival Model (MSM) for mixtures with differing action, and the Additive Dose Model (ADM) for mixtures with similar action.

• The **Multiplicative Survival, MSM** (or Independent Action, IA) models assume that the effects of active ingredients originate from different modes of action, where independent action implies there is no interaction between the active ingredients. These models propose that the individual effects of the ingredients should be multiplied together to estimate the overall effect of their combination. They tend to be more simple to perform, and are often preferred for patents and discovery trials. However, this model is subject to errors arising from the nonlinear nature of the dose-response curve, if the active ingredients are compared at rates outside the linear phase of the curve.

• The **Additive Dose, ADM** (or concentration addition, CA) models assume that the combined effects of active ingredients arise from similar modes of action (i.e. the active ingredients may target the same biological pathway or process but can have subtle differences in their specific molecular targets or modes of interaction (i.e. bind differently to the same target sites, and/or differ in potency). These models assume interaction between the active ingredients, and propose that the effects of individual ingredients can be added together to predict the overall effect of their combination. They tend to be more complex to perform, and are often preferred for development trials, where the ratio optimization is required.

Model	Assumptions	Analysis	Comment
Multiplicative Survival Model (MSM)	Assumes effects originate from different modes of action. Based on % mortality.	Abbot's formula (= Limpel's formula or Colby's method)	(+) Rapid and simple: does not require multiple doses / dose-response curves (and thus less experimental work) to predict expected responses. (-) Subject to errors arising from the nonlinear nature of the dose-response curve
Additive Dose Model (ADM)	Assumes effects originate from similar modes. Based on observed effective concentrations (e.g., EC50).	Wadley's method Tammes method Co-toxicity method	(-) Slower and more complex: requires multiple doses / dose response curves for EC50 determination (more experimental work) (+) Avoids errors arising from the nonlinear nature of the dose-response curve (+) optimization of mix ratios for maximal synergy

The choice between these models depends on the underlying assumption about the relationship between the modes of action of the active ingredients.

If the active ingredients are known to act in a similar manner, such as targeting the same biological process or pathway, the ADM models are more appropriate. Conversely, if the active ingredients are known to act through different mechanisms or pathways, the MSM models would be more suitable.

When evaluating mixes of active ingredients with similar modes of action, there may be instances where using the simpler Multiplicative Survival (MSM) models can be justified:

• During the initial screening or early stages of research, where the primary objective is to identify potential combinations for further investigation, the simpler models can serve as a starting point. These models allow for a quick assessment of the effects of the active ingredients and can guide decision-making on which combinations warrant more detailed examination.

• Using more complex models that account for interactions between active ingredients may require additional data, resources, or expertise. If these requirements are not readily available or feasible, adopting the MSM as a pragmatic approach can provide reasonable estimates of the combined effects.

However, it is important to note that while the MSM models offer simplicity and practicality, they may oversimplify complex biological interactions.

If there is evidence or strong indications of interaction or synergy between the active ingredients, employing more sophisticated models or conducting additional studies to explore these interactions would be necessary for a comprehensive assessment.

The synergy ratio (R)

To determine synergy, the synergy ratio (R) is calculated. If the experimentally observed efficacy of a mix of two active ingredients A and B (A+B$\underline{o}$) is greater than the expected, calculated expected efficacy (A+B$\underline{e}$) then synergy (R>1) is exhibited.

	Mathematical definition (MSM)	Biological definition (ADM)
Synergistic	R>1	R>1,5
Additive	R=1	R =0,5-1,5
Antagonistic	R<1	R<0,5

If R=1 then the effect is additive and if R<1 then antagonism is exhibited. For the more conservative MSM model (for patents and discovery trials, where the cost of a false negative is high), potential synergies are accounted for more cautiously, and the mathematical definition is used and accepted, while for ADM models (for development trials, where the cost of a false positive is high) a more stringent biological definition is generally used.

———

23

MULTIPLICATIVE SURVIVAL MODEL (MSM) FOR ACTIVE INGREDIENTS WITH DIFFERING MODES OF ACTION

In crop protection R&D, the Multiplicative Survival Model (MSM) for active ingredients with differing modes of action is most encountered (particularly in the patent literature), because they do not require multiple doses (and thus less experimental work) to predict expected responses.

Colby's method for binary mixes

In the following, we will refer to this method as Colby's method, as it is the most used name (despite Abbot's formula predating Limpel and Colby's later analysis of the method).

Colby's method is typically used in patent applications to provide a relatively simple demonstration of the interaction between active ingredients in a mixture (additivity, synergism, or antagonism).

For Colby's equation, calculations for synergy are best given from data where the requirement of dose-response linearity (generally considered to be within the range of 20% and 80% efficacy) is fulfilled - at higher rates the accuracy of synergy calculation is compromised due to the flattening of the dose-response curve at the upper asymptote. For Colby's equation, calculations for synergy are thus best given from data where the individual active ingredients, as well as the mixture, have been applied at a dose providing between 20-80% (ideally no more than 50%) control, since the requirement of dose-response linearity is fulfilled in this range.

In the Colby method, for a given combination of two active components, E (expected efficacy) can be expressed as:

$$E = A + B - \left(\frac{AB}{100}\right)$$

where E = expected efficacy, A and B = the efficacy of two active ingredients A and B at a given dose.

Example, Colby's method for binary mixes:

100g/Ha of active ingredients A kills 30% of the weeds, 75g/Ha of B kills 50% of the weeds. If 100g of A kills 30% of the weeds, then there are 70% remaining. The best that adding 75g of B can expect to achieve is 40% of the remaining 70%. i.e., A+B(expected) =30+(40*70/100) = 58. If A+B (observed) is > A+B (expected) then synergy (R>1) is exhibited. If R=1 then the effect is additive and if R<1 then antagonism is exhibited:

100g/Ha	75g/Ha	100+75g/Ha		
A	B	A+B (o)	A+B(e)	R
30	40	80	58	1,38

In this example the observed efficacy is 80% for the mix of A+B, and the synergism ratio (R) between observed and expected is 1,38. The mix of A+B is synergistic. Coby's method can also be represented graphically as:

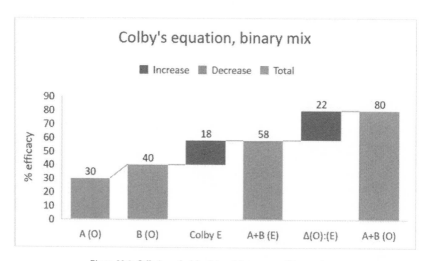

Figure 23.1: Colby's method for determining synergy, binary mixes.

1.2. Colby's method for ternary mixes

The MSM model for three active ingredients with differing modes of action is less commonly encountered. For a given combination of three active components, E (expected efficacy) can be calculated as:

$$E = A + B + C - \left(\frac{AB + AC + BC}{100}\right) + \left(\frac{ABC}{10000}\right)$$

where E = expected efficacy, A, B and C = the efficacy of three active ingredients A, B and C at a given dose.

When the percentage of control observed for the combination is greater than the expected percentage, there is a synergistic effect - the synergism ratio (R) is calculated as the ratio between the expected values and observed values.

If the synergism ratio (R) between observed and expected is >1 then synergy is exhibited, if R=1 then the effect is additive and if R<1 then the mix is antagonistic.

Example, Colby's method for ternary mixes:

1kg/Ha of active ingredients A kills 20% of the weeds, 1kg/Ha of B kills 30% of the weeds and 1kg/Ha of C kills 35% of the weeds. If A+B+C (observed) is > A+B+C (expected) then synergy (R>1) is exhibited. If R=1 then the effect is additive and if R<1 then antagonism is exhibited:

1kg	1kg	1kg	1+1+1=3kg	A+B+C (e)	R
A	B	C	A+B+C (o)		
20	30	35	80	64	1,26

In this example, the observed efficacy is 80% for the mix of A+B+C, and the synergism ratio (R) between observed and expected is 1,26. The mix of A+B+C is synergistic. The MSM method for ternary mixes with differing modes of action can also be represented graphically as:

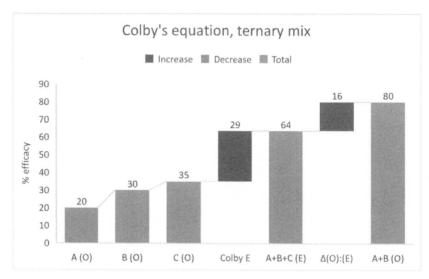

Figure 23.2: Colby's method for determining synergy, ternary mixes.

24

ADDITIVE DOSE MODEL (ADM) FOR ACTIVE INGREDIENTS WITH SIMILAR MODES OF ACTION

A more accurate (but less common, as it requires more experimental work) determination of the interaction between active ingredients in a mixture can be made by the Additive Dose Model (ADM).

The ADM method assumes that effects originate from similar modes of action, and that one component can substitute at a constant ratio for the other (the "equally effective rate").

The expected effectiveness of a mixture A+B(e) can thus be predicted from the effectiveness of the individual active ingredients when their relative ratio is known.

Example, equally effective rates:

In this example, the EC50 of active ingredient A is experimentally determined as 250g/Ha, the EC50 of active ingredient B is 0,9g/Ha.

In a mix, A and B substitute for each other at a constant ratio to give an "equally effective rate" – for example in mix 2 (below): a mix of A+B where 50% of A (125g ai/Ha) is replaced by 50% of B (0,45g ai/Ha).

The "weight ratio" is defined as the ratio of the individual active ingredient (A or B) to the mix (A+B). Examples of other ratios are given in the following, and will be the basis of the following method examples:

"Equally effective" rates, A+B (g ai/Ha)

Mix	AI	Ratio	g ai/Ha	Weight ratio
1	A	75%	188	99,9%
1	B	25%	0,23	0,1%
2	A	50%	125	99,6%
2	B	50%	0,45	0,4%
3	A	25%	63	98,9%
3	B	75%	0,68	1,1%

Wadley's method for binary mixes

Wadley's method is based on EC50 values (effective concentration required to obtain a 50% effect) typically derived by linear or non-linear regression from dose-response experiments, and thus avoids errors arising from the nonlinear nature of the dose-response curve.

In the Wadley method, for a given combination of two active components, E (expected EC50) can be expressed as:

$$E = \frac{(a+b)}{\frac{a}{EC50(Ao)} + \frac{b}{EC50(Bo)}}$$

where a and b are the weight ratios (EC50 values in g/Ha) of compound A and B in the mixture and EC50(Ao) and EC50(Bo) are the experimentally observed (o) EC50 values obtained using the dose response curves for the individual compounds.

The synergism ratio (R) is calculated as the ratio between the expected values and observed values, EC50 A+B(e)/EC50 A+B(o).

Example, Wadley's method for binary mixes:

The EC50 of active ingredient A is experimentally determined as 250g/Ha, the EC50 of active ingredient B is 0,9g/Ha. In a mix, A and B substitute for each other at a constant ratio where 50% of A (125g ai/Ha) is replaced by 50% of B (0,45g ai/Ha).

The EC50 is 70 g ai/Ha for the mix of A+B. If A+B (observed) is > A+B (expected) then synergy (R>1) is exhibited. If R=1 then the effect is additive and if R<1 then antagonism is exhibited:

EC50	EC50	EC50	EC50	R	Weight ratio	
A(o)	B(o)	A+B(o)	A+B(e)		a	b
250	0,9	70	125,45	1,79	99,64	0,36

In this example, the observed EC50 is 70 g ai/Ha for the mix of A+B and the synergism factor (R) between observed and expected is 1,79. The mix of A+B is synergistic.

One objective of studying synergy is to maximize the cost/benefit ratio of active ingredients in a mix, to attain maximal efficacy with minimal active ingredient.

Wadley's method can be used to evaluate multiple "equally effective rate" ratios (see above):

EC50	EC50	EC50	EC50	R	Weight ratio	
A(o)	B(o)	A+B(o)	A+B(e)		a	b
250	0,90	110	187,73	1,71	99,9%	0,1%
250	0,90	70	125,45	1,79	99,6%	0,4%
250	0,90	40	63,18	1,58	98,9%	1,1%

In this example, the synergy ratio (R=1,79) is greatest for the 50:50 mix, with A and B substituting for each other at a constant ratio where 50% of A (125g ai/Ha) is replaced by 50% of B (0,45g ai/Ha).

Wadley's method for ternary mixes

For ternary (three component) mixes, Wadley's theoretical or expected model may be rewritten as:

$$E = \frac{(a + b + c)}{\frac{a}{EC50(Ao)} + \frac{b}{EC50(Bo)} + \frac{c}{EC50(Co)}}$$

where a, b and c are the weight ratios (ratio of EC50 values in g/Ha) of compounds A, B and C in the mixture and EC50(Ao), EC50(Bo) and EC50(Co) are the experimentally observed (o) EC50 values obtained using the dose response curves for the individual compounds.

The synergism ratio (R) is calculated as the ratio between the expected values and observed values, EC50 A+B+C(e)/EC50 A+B+C(o).

Isobole method for binary mixes and multiple dose ratios

The Isobole method (also called Tammes method) is an extension of the Wadley method and uses a graphic representation to determine the effect of multiple dose ratios on the level of synergistic effect, to determine the mix ratio at which the greatest synergy is observed.

Like the Wadley method, the Tammes method is based on EC50 values and avoids errors arising from the nonlinear nature of the dose-response curve.

Example, Isobole method for binary mixes with multiple dose ratios:

In this example, the EC50 of active ingredient A is experimentally determined as 250g/Ha, the EC50 of active ingredient B is 0,9g/Ha. In a mix, A and B substitute for each other at a constant ratio to give an "equally effective rate" – for example in mix 3 (below): a mix of A+B where 50% of A (125g ai/Ha) is replaced by 50% of B (0,45g ai/Ha).

The EC50s are used to plan a factorial trial with 25 treatments / 50 rates (g ai/Ha) comprising five rates (0,25X to 4X) and five mix ratios (100:0; 75:25; 50:50; 25:75; 0:100):

Mix	AI	Ratio	"Equally effective" rate, A+B (g ai/Ha)				
			4x	2x	1x	0,5x	0,25x
1	A	100%	1000	500	250	125	63
	B	0%	0	0	0	0	0
2	A	75%	750	375	188	94	47
	B	25%	0,90	0,45	0,23	0,11	0,06
3	A	50%	500	250	125	63	31
	B	50%	1,80	0,90	0,45	0,23	0,11
4	A	25%	250	125	63	31	16
	B	75%	2,70	1,35	0,68	0,34	0,17
5	A	0%	0	0	0	0	0
	B	100%	3,60	1,80	0,90	0,45	0,23

The factorial trial with 25 treatments is carried out and EC50 values are determined by e.g. nonlinear regression for each mix ratio, and the EC50s for each AI are calculated as a factor of their weight ratios (e.g. for mix 3 (above), the rates 250 : 0,9g ai/Ha corresponds to a ratio of 99,6 : 0,4%).

The outcome of mix 3 corresponds to the example given earlier for Wadley's method - the observed EC50 is 70 g ai/Ha for the "equally effective dose" of A+B (where 50% of A (125g ai/Ha) is replaced by 50% of B (0,45g ai/Ha).

Finally, the EC50s for each AI are plotted as an isobole (a plot in rectangular coordinates where the axes represent the doses of active ingredient A and B):

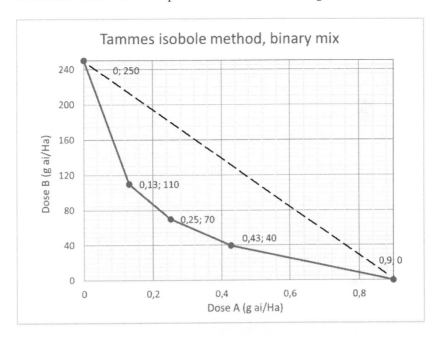

The dotted straight line represents the EC50 isobole for an expected additive effect (additive isobole) of differing "equally effective" ratios of A and B, while the curved full line represents the actual experimental EC50s for the specified mixture ratios.

If mixture EC50s are positioned below the additive isobole (as they are here) they are considered synergistic (synergistic isobole), and if the mixtures are positioned above, they are considered antagonistic (antagonistic isobole).

The mix ratio with the greatest distance from the isobole (in this example mix 3) has the greatest synergy. This corresponds to the Wadley analysis, where the synergy ratio (R=1,79) was greatest for the 50:50 mi, with A and B substituting for each other at a constant ratio where 50% of A (125g ai/Ha) is replaced by 50% of B (0,45g ai/Ha).

Co-toxicity model for binary mixes

A further method occasionally encountered in the literature is that of co-toxicity model. The outcome on the same dataset is the same as for the Wadley model (see below).

In contrast to the Wadley model, this model is based on converting EC50 values for the individual active ingredients and the mix to a toxicity index (TI):

$$TI(A) \ compared \ to \ B \ as \ the \ standard = \frac{EC50(A)}{EC50(B)} * 100$$

$$TI(B) compared \ to \ B \ as \ the \ standard = \frac{EC50(A)}{EC50(B)} * 100$$

$$Observed \ TI(A + B) = \frac{EC50(A)}{EC50(A + B)} * 100$$

$$Theoretical \ TI(A + B) = [TI(A) * \% \ of \ A \ in \ mix] + [TI(B) * \% \ of \ B \ in \ mix]$$

The cotoxicity coefficient (CC) of the mix can then be calculated as:

$$CC(A + B) = \frac{TI(A + B) \ observed}{TI(A + B) \ theoretical}$$

When the cotoxicity coefficient (CC) of the mix is greater than 100, there is a synergistic effect. If the CC equals 100 then the effect is additive and if less than 100, antagonism is exhibited).

Example, co-toxicity method for binary mixes:

The EC50 of active ingredient A is experimentally determined as 250g/Ha, the EC50 of active ingredient B is 0,9g/Ha and the EC50 is 70 g ai/Ha for the mix of A+B.

The theoretical toxicity index for the mix is 0,72 and the observed toxicity index for the mix is 1,3, giving a cotoxicity coefficient (CC) of the mix of 179:

EC50	EC50	EC50	Cotoxicity coefficient	R	Weight ratio		Toxicity index (TI)		Toxicity index (A+B)	
A(o)	B(o)	A+B(o)	CC(A+B)		a	b	TI(A)	TI(B)	Observed	Theoretical
250	0,9	70	179	1,79	99,64	0,36	0,36	100	1,3	0,72

This outcome again corresponds to the example given earlier for Wadley's method - for both methods (Wadley and co-toxicity) the synergism factor (R) between observed and expected is 1,79 and the mix of A+B is synergistic.

———

PLEASE LEAVE A REVIEW

Thanks for reading GUIDE TO ESSENTIAL BIOSTATISTICS! Your support makes it possible for this author to continue creating.

If what you read provided value, **please leave an honest review** wherever you bought this book. Your feedback is invaluable, and reviews help new readers discover my work.

———

To get in touch with me directly, please use one of the various contact methods listed at:

http://biocomm.eu

Made in the USA
Columbia, SC
11 August 2023

21502867R00107